Into Our Third Century Series

FROM EVERY NATION WITHOUT NUMBER:

RACIAL AND ETHNIC DIVERSITY IN UNITED METHODISM

ROY I. SANO

Alan K. Waltz, Editor

ABINGDON
Nashville

FROM EVERY NATION WITHOUT NUMBER:
Racial and Ethnic Diversity in United Methodism

Library of Congress Cataloging in Publication Data

SANO, ROY I. (ROY ISAO), 1931-
 From every nation without number.
 (Into our third century)
 Includes bibliographical references.
 1. United Methodist Church (U.S.)—Membership. 2. Church and
 race relations—Methodist Church.
 I. Waltz, Alan K. II. Title. III. Series.
 BX8382.2.Z5S36   287'.6   81-20610   AACR2

ISBN 0-687-13642-3 (pbk.)

MANUFACTURED BY THE PARTHENON PRESS AT
NASHVILLE, TENNESSEE, UNITED STATES OF AMERICA

To

Bishop Donald Harvey Tippett
and
in loving memory of his wife, Ruth

Contents

Foreword

In 1984 The United Methodist Church will observe its two hundredth anniversary. The Christmas Conference of 1784 is most often regarded as the formal beginning of the Methodist movement in the United States. This historic meeting adopted the Articles of Religion, established a polity, elected Thomas Coke and Francis Asbury as superintendents, consecrated Asbury at the hands of Philip Otterbein and others, took other organizational steps and called for a rebirth of evangelism and scriptural holiness in the new nation.

The observance of the bicentennial of The United Methodist Church is a time when we pause to reflect upon how the Wesleyan vision of holy love and vital piety spread throughout the nation. In the report of the Bicentennial Planning Committee approved at the 1980 General Conference we have these words. "As we approach the end of our second century, we look forward with excitement and hope to the beginning of a third century in the service of our Lord. Our concern is that, through our recognition of the past and our affirmation of the present, we will be called into the future as new beings, refreshed by our experience of

Christ, revived in our commitments to bring salvation, peace and justice to all of God's children, and renewed as a people of God in our own time."

The occasion of the bicentennial is a time soberly to anticipate the future and carefully to assess ourselves as we move into our third century. Our inheritance is one of great achievements. We have seen periods of great expansion in our denomination and we are now experiencing a time of contraction and retrenchment. Yet the challenge and vision are still present, to serve in the name of Christ and to spread the call to salvation and spiritual rebirth. We need to experience anew the sense of mission and purpose which filled our forebears with the power to evangelize a nation.

Again we turn to the words of the report of the Bicentennial Planning Committee to General Conference. "The future is a time for new birth and our Bicentennial prayer will be a call to new birth of the fervent spirit of Methodism, to a new birth of personal obedience to the Christ, to a new birth of creative local congregations, to a new birth of evangelical zeal, and to a new birth of our vital commitment to peace and social justice."

As a United Methodist lay member or pastor, you and your congregation have a significant role in both the celebration and in the search for and the making possible of the new birth in our denomination. It is the people in the pews and pulpits of United Methodism who must reestablish our identity and purpose and infuse it with the excitement and commitment to bring its mission to fruition. We believe that through the thorough examination of who we are as United

Methodists, what we want to accomplish and how we choose to pursue our goals, we will find the renewed purpose and vision to complete our task in the name of Christ.

Into Our Third Century, a series of books initiated by the General Council on Ministries with the encouragement of the Council of Bishops, is intended to assist your reflection on and discussion of the issues confronting The United Methodist Church. The books are based on individually commissioned studies and research projects. Over a four-year period, beginning in 1980, seventeen separate volumes are being released. The present book, *From Every Nation Without Number,* is the eleventh volume in the series. Books already published are listed opposite the title page. Others scheduled for release deal with the professional ministry, financial support, social movements and issues, outreach ministries and polity.

The General Council on Ministries is pleased to commend to you this book by Roy I. Sano. The book deals with the issues related to the racial and ethnic diversity within The United Methodist Church. It describes the historic and present-day contributions of the racial and ethnic minorities to the life of the denomination. Dr. Sano provides a conceptual framework to help us understand the theological and social issues in relationships between minority and majority groups. We are helped to understand the unity which we are to find within the Christian community and how we are to enable this unity in God to come into fruition in our lives and in our denomination. Through our individual lives and in our local congregations we are

challenged to move to the fullness of the unity of all
peoples in Christ.

We hope that you will share your response and
reactions to this book with others in your congregation.
Discuss it with district, conference, and general church
leaders. Explore with the author the issues raised. Your
response will also be welcomed by the members and
staff of the General Council on Ministries.

Norman E. Dewire
General Secretary

Alan K. Waltz
Editor

General Council on Ministries
601 West Riverview Avenue
Dayton, Ohio 45406

April, 1982

CHAPTER 1

Goal of The United Methodist Church: Racial Inclusiveness

The church on earth should reflect our vision of heaven as described in Revelation where there will be "a great multitude, which no one could count, from every nation and all tribes and peoples and tongues, standing before the throne and before the Lamb" (Rev. 7:9 NAS).

The vision of Christ's church here and now for United Methodists, as stated in the denominational constitution, directs that

> The United Methodist Church is a part of the Church Universal, which is one Body in Christ. Therefore all persons, without regard to race, color, national origin, or economic condition, shall be eligible to attend its worship services, to participate in its programs, and, when they take the appropriate vows, to be admitted into its membership in any local church in the connection. In The United Methodist Church no conference or other organizational unit of the Church shall be structured so as to exclude any member or any constituent body of the Church because of race, color, national origin, or economic condition.[1]

Is The United Methodist Church fulfilling God's will and living up to its own constitutional mandate? It appears that we have a long way to go to attain our aspirations. A 1974 study by Alan Waltz revealed that ethnic and racial minorities comprised 4.3 percent of the total membership of The United Methodist Church, while the national profile showed that ethnic and racial minorities made upward of 20 percent of the population.[2]

The disparity between our aspirations and the limited number of ethnic minorities in The United Methodist Church raises several questions: (1) can we expect a significant presence of racial and ethnic minorities within The United Methodist Church? (2) what factors influence the racial composition of the denomination? (3) how might we proceed if we are to conduct an effective ethnic minority ministry? These are the questions this book will consider.

The survey conducted in connection with the preparation of this book indicated that if we are to make a realistic estimate of those prospects, we must first examine social and psychological factors influencing attempts to attain racial and ethnic inclusiveness in The United Methodist Church. Only then can we explore concrete steps that will lead to the attainment of our goal.

Today few whites, who comprise the overwhelming majority in The United Methodist Church, have firsthand knowledge or sustained interaction with racial and ethnic minorities. Except for a few who have occasion to move outside their enclaves and outposts, the white membership has little opportunity to question or correct the shocking and soothing images of colorful peoples used by the media to sell news and entertainment. Ethnic minorities and their counterparts in the

Third World are therefore perceived as threats or depicted in unrealistically exotic and romantic terms. In either case, social distance minimizes communication. We will examine local churches within The United Methodist Church as they move toward the goal of communication and cooperation.

Our survey was taken in 1980. Questionnaires formulated by a team of consultants were sent to a divergent group of people within the denomination representing various racial and ethnic groups—whites, blacks, Hispanic Americans, American Indians, and Pacific and Asian Americans. Respondents to the survey included both laity and clergy, from various regions of the country. The consultants analyzed responses to the survey for significant issues raised, deep aspirations expressed, and rich experiences retold. Our study was built upon these responses. After reviewing the first draft of the study, the same consultants offered additional suggestions, many of which were incorporated into the study. While we have thus attempted to make this study responsive to the concerns and aspirations of a wide range of persons in The United Methodist Church, the study inevitably remains predominantly a statement by an individual.

Our exploration of the prospects for racial minorities in the denomination encompasses four steps. First we will briefly review relevant historical highlights reflecting efforts within and accomplishments by The United Methodist Church toward racial and ethnic inclusiveness. In chapters 3 and 4 we will discuss cultural, sociological, and psychological dynamics influencing hopes for race relations in The United Methodist

Church. In chapters 5 and 6 we will reflect on the issues of race from a perspective of faith, and consider insights from our faith which bear on the challenges uncovered. In chapter 7 we will consider concrete steps toward making The United Methodist Church a truly inclusive church and a force capable of influencing events. Our focus will be on the local church, for, in the words of the late Bishop A. Raymond Grant:

> The problem of racial segregation infects Methodism at every level of its institutional life, and plans are afoot for its removal. Nowhere is the problem more agonizingly stubborn, however, than at the local church level. Racial segregation in the church rests ultimately on the foundation of racial prejudice in the people, but that foundation is also strengthened by the institutional segregation which has been built upon it. The point at which these two, personal prejudice and institutional segregation, come together most directly is in the local congregation.[5]

I am especially indebted to the panel of consultants for their participation in and contributions to this study. These persons are Ignacio Castuera, Douglass E. Fitch, Ezra Earl Jones, Kathleen A. Thomas-Sano, and Becky Thompson. In addition, Kathleen A. Thomas-Sano served as the coordinator for the total project. Support and assistance were given by others as well. Ezra Earl Jones and Alan K. Waltz have served as the liaison persons with the General Council on Ministries, the sponsors of the project. Carol Evans Smith assisted with the editing of the manuscript; Lola Conrad typed the final manuscript for publication. Deep appreciation is also expressed to all who responded to the question-naires and interviews and who shared their concerns, insights, and stories.

CHAPTER 2

The Ends in Our Beginnings

In surveying the past, we restrict ourselves to beginning points of major historic developments toward the goals related to our queries. We find positive signs which point to our goals or "ends in our beginnings." A day-by-day log of our journey will not be found here, only suggestive landmarks from our records which point to two simple facts: (1) the involvement of ethnic minorities in The United Methodist Church has been long and varied, and (2) considerable progress is needed for ethnic inclusiveness to be realized.

A. THE RECORD

1. The Wesleys

Any glance into the historic moments of The United Methodist Church includes a look at John and Charles Wesley, whose work among American Indians was a natural development within their spiritual pilgrimage. Despite the fact that this early stage of their ministry, before 1738, has been regarded in lowly terms, the fact remains that from the earliest days of the Wesleys' ministry, missionary work among Native Americans was seen as part of their calling.

2. Early Ethnic Minority Members

From the earliest days of the United Methodist heritage in the United States, the black presence was conspicuous. Negroes were included in the two earliest known organized bodies of Methodism on this continent. In 1764 Robert Strawbridge organized in a log cabin in Frederick County, Maryland, what is regarded by many as the first Methodist society in the New World. Among the members of the first class roll was Anne, a black slave of the Switzer family. When a class was organized on John Street in New York City in 1766, one of the five charter members was a black slave woman named Betty. Through the impact of this fellowship, which later became Wesley Chapel on John Street, other groups were organized, so that "within six months, about twenty-four persons received justifying grace, near half of them whites, and the rest negroes."[1]

3. Early Ethnic Minority Preachers:
Landmarks of Wholeness

Black preachers were also among the early leaders of the movement. Among them was Harry Hoosier, or "Black Harry," who accompanied Francis Asbury on his extensive travels. Dr. Thomas Coke, the first bishop of the Methodist movement in England, called Black Harry "one of the best preachers in the world." Dr. Benjamin Rush, a signer of the Declaration of Independence and a prominent Philadelphia resident, said that Harry Hoosier was "the greatest orator in America."[2]

In attending the Christmas Conference in 1784 in Baltimore, at which the Methodist Episcopal Church was organized, Black Harry was joined by another black preacher, Richard Allen, who was a slave at the time. After purchasing his freedom, in 1799 Mr. Allen became the first Negro to be officially ordained in the ministry of The Methodist Episcopal Church. Mistreatment suffered by his people led him to organize the African Methodist Episcopal Church, which remains a separate denomination today.[3]

Perhaps Richard Allen's presence at the Christmas Conference foreshadows a union yet to come, in the same way as did the presence of German-speaking Philip William Otterbein at that conference. In 1800 Otterbein organized the United Brethren in Christ, which merged with the Evangelical Association in 1946. It joined The Methodist Church and created The United Methodist Church in 1968.

A free-born Negro from Virginia named Harry Evans symbolizes an early expression of our aspirations for an inclusive church. By trade a cobbler, he became an itinerant local preacher after his conversion in Delaware. A church he started in Fayetteville, North Carolina, became a racially inclusive congregation, and eventually had more white members than black.[4]

John Stewart symbolizes the place of racially mixed persons and inter-ethnic accord. A free-born mulatto working among Indians, he is considered the "first home missionary" within the Wesleyan branch of United Methodist heritage. Driven to poverty and alcoholism by lack of work, he was contemplating suicide in 1814 when he was drawn to a camp meeting and converted by a Methodist preacher. He began work among Indians in November, 1816, using an interpreter to communicate. Among his first converts were four tribal chiefs, two of whom became local preachers. By 1822 his mission to the Wyandot had two hundred members. He died in 1828 at the age of thirty-seven, while serving a circuit with a five-hundred-mile circumference.[5]

John and Charles Wesley, "Black Harry," Richard Allen, Philip William Otterbein, Harry Evans, John Stewart—in their way, these people stand as landmarks of a wholeness that is integral to the vision of the movement's early days.

4. Ministry of White Leaders:
   The Missionary Movement

Ethnic minorities were not alone in promoting an inclusive body of Christ within the United Methodist heritage. Many white leaders worked for wholeness within the community of faith by bringing into the fellowship of believers a diversity of people. They took strong stands against the racial abuses of their day and launched campaigns against impediments which thwarted God's work of salvation. They were thus reaching out to give visible evidence that "the earth is the Lord's and the fulness thereof" (Ps. 24:1). This comprehensive form of ministry among white leaders is illustrated best in the missionary movement, the major ingredients of which were evangelism, social justice, and education.

a. *Evangelism.* "I look upon the whole world as my parish." John Wesley thus responded to criticism of his preaching as an Anglican clergy in a parish to which he had not been invited or assigned. "Go out and preach the Gospel to all the world," he told Dr. Thomas Coke, who was ousted from a pastorate in the Church of England when his sympathies for the Wesleyan revivals were discovered.

Later as a general superintendent of the Methodist movement, Dr. Coke presided at the 1784 Christmas Conference in North America and inspired the sending of missionaries to Nova Scotia and the West Indies. He wrote *A History of the West Indies* (1809-11), vigorously resisted slave trade, and encouraged work in Sierra Leone. As early as 1784, nine years before William Carey's departure signaled the beginning of the modern missionary movement, Dr. Coke urged a missionary effort in India. He volunteered for work in Sri Lanka, formerly Ceylon, but died enroute in 1814.[6]

Missionary efforts which began in gestures by local groups were later sponsored by conferences. Various traditions which comprise The United Methodist Church eventually organized denominational societies. Separate societies were led and supported by women in the denominations. Through these efforts, Hispanics, Asians, Africans, American Indians, and Island people became part of the consciousness and membership of various denominations, contributing in some small measure toward an inclusive Body of Christ.

b. *Social Justice.* The missionary effort was concerned not only with saving the soul, but also with liberating the total person from bondage. One of the most vivid illustrations appears in the struggle against slavery. As in the missionary endeavor, the story may be mixed, but the authentic word is still heard: people in this heritage worked for emancipation of slavery.

In 1743 John Wesley produced the "General Rules of Our United Societies," which reminded members to do no harm, such as "buying or selling of men, women, and children with an intention to enslave them."[7] In 1774 John Wesley wrote his famous essay, "Thoughts upon Slavery." The 1780 Conference of American societies stated concrete measures to eliminate slavery from their midst.

> Does this Conference acknowledge that slavery is contrary to the laws of God, man, and nature, and hurtful to society; contrary to the dictates of conscience and pure religion, and doing that which we would not others should do to us and ours? Do we pass our disapprobation on all our friends . . . who keep slaves, and advise their freedom? . . . Yes. Ought not this Conference to require those travelling preachers who hold slaves to give promise to set them free? Yes.[8]

The struggle against slavery and oppression appears in other parts of our heritage. The Evangelical Association, in its General Conference of 1847, stated: "None of our members shall be permitted to hold slaves or traffic in them under any pretext whatever."[9] The United Brethren Church, at a meeting of its missionary society in 1879, resolved, "That the unjust discrimination becoming so general in this country against negroes, Indians, Chinese, and all who have mixed blood, is criminal before God and a shame to our Christian civilization."[10]

c. *Education.* Once people were free, cultivating their best potentials was a major concern. The work of the Freedmen's Aid Society in establishing schools at various levels beginning in 1866, stands as a remarkable record enshrined in the twelve black United Methodist colleges today.[11] The Navajo Methodist School in Farmington, New Mexico, was established for Native Americans, as was the Lydia Patterson School in El Paso, Texas, for Mexican Americans. Loans and scholarships aided the development of blacks, Hispanics, Native Americans, and Pacific and Asian Americans, many of whom have given conspicuous leadership in the church.

5. Organizational Efforts Among Racial Minorities:
   Past and Present Trends

Diverse organizational efforts among racial minorities have appeared within the several strands of our heritage. Ethnic minority local churches were launched, followed by the establishment of supportive structures beyond the local level. Under the movement for integration in the twentieth century, however, most of these structures, such as the early missionary and provisional conferences and the Central Jurisdiction for blacks, were reduced in number. Today in the United States only the Oklahoma Indian Missionary Conference and the Rio Grande Annual Conference remain.

With the resurgence of ethnic consciousness in the late 1960s and early 1970s came the establishment of various ethnic caucuses such as the Black Methodists for Church Renewal, MARCHA (Methodists Associated Representing the Cause of Hispanic Americans), the National Federation of Asian American United Methodists, and the Native American International Committee. Although these organizations lack disciplinary or official status, some boards, agencies, and Annual Conferences work with them on a wide range of the church's work in evangelism, education, worship, social services, and missions. While these developments may not lead to the reestablishment of ethnically distinct disciplinary structures, *new forms beyond these informal, ad hoc arrangements are yet to be articulated.* The caucuses and ethnic conferences are now moving the church into modes of work which have not been fully clarified, partly because of the fluidity and the variety of direction which the movements of the Spirit are taking.

B. THE RESULTS

1. 1974 Waltz Survey

What have these early visions and long struggles produced to date? Dr. Alan K. Waltz, of the General Council on Ministries of The United Methodist Church, conducted a survey of ethnic minority membership in the denomination in 1973, which remains to date "the only count of ethnic minority membership totals."[12] According to his data, 11.1 percent of local United Methodist churches had ethnic minority members. Of these, 69 percent were predominantly "ethnic minority local churches" having 50 percent or more ethnic minority members. Ethnic minorities comprised 4.3 percent of the total membership of The United Methodist Church. Of these, blacks constituted 86.5 percent. Ninety-two percent of the ethnic minority members belong to predominantly ethnic minority local churches.

Two major conclusions can be drawn from Dr. Waltz's survey:

a. *Much Work Remains for The United Methodist Church.* The United Methodist Church had less than 5 percent ethnic minority membership when the national profile showed ethnic minorities made upward of 20 percent of the population.

b. *Key Tool: Predominantly Ethnic Minority Local Church.* Ethnic minority membership is concentrated in predominantly *ethnic minority local churches.* Thus, it appears that these churches *represent the most effective evangelistic method* the denomination has to promote an inclusive membership.

2. Ethnically Defined Structures Beyond the Local
    Church: Potential Importance

The distinct role of the ethnic minority local church was affirmed by the present survey, and is treated in more depth in chapters 3 and 7. The resurgence of ethnic consciousness and the formation of makeshift ethnic organizations point to the potential importance of ethnically defined institutions beyond the local church. Let us keep in mind these potentially key tools, as well as the lingering hope for constructive contributions by white and multiracial congregations.

CHAPTER 3

Beyond the Melting Pot: A Two-Category System

A. DISTINCT ETHNIC STRUCTURES IN THE DENOMINATION

1. Ethnic Minority Support

Our predominantly white denomination has worked with its ethnic minorities by creating both (1) separate institutions for racial minorities, such as local churches, educational institutions, and conferences, and (2) subgroups within organizations, such as units addressing ethnic issues in conferences or boards and agencies.

Although findings of our present survey represent broad trends, and opinions are not neatly divided along ethnic lines, the responses suggest an interesting contrast. Racial and ethnic minorities, the people directly affected by separate structures and subgroups within the denomination, favor ethnic minority local churches, and are open to ethnically defined structures beyond the local church, such as subgroups or staff positions within general boards and agencies, and, in some cases, conference-like structures.

2. White Opposition

Whites, on the other hand, tend to look negatively toward distinct arrangements for ethnic minorities.

Some regard ethnic conferences within the continental United States (such as those created for Native American work in Oklahoma and for Mexican Americans along the Rio Grande River) and even ethnic minority local churches, as a necessary concession to human weakness or social evil. Others look upon such arrangements as serious departures from the Christian faith, which should be eliminated as soon as possible.

It is noteworthy that the negative response detected among the white constituency represents the overwhelming majority of our denomination. Hence, the white majority is in a position to decide the fate of an ethnic constituency contrary to their aspirations, or at best to tolerate as a nuisance or embarrassment structures which ethnic minorities are likely to favor.

What lies behind this negative reaction? Is it appropriate to our situation? This chapter will focus on these questions.

B. UNITY AT THE EXPENSE OF DISTINCTIVENESS?

1. E Pluribus Unum: A Political Philosophy with a Religious Aura

"Why can't ethnic minorities join existing organizations and be like whites?" No wonder this question is asked, when the religious aura of our political philosophy has influenced the theology of our church. Our vision of an ideal church and society is a nation and a denomination where unity prevails. But are our hopes for the church being shaped by a misapplied cultural force rather than by the Word of God—a cultural force traceable to a fundamental value forged in our origins and at the time of testing?

After our Republic nearly relapsed into the clutches of the Old World because the Articles of Confederation were inept, we secured our place in the world with a Federal Constitution. The change was captured in the motto, e pluribus unum, meaning "from many one." The overriding emphasis of that time was the elimination of differences among colonies and the establishment of unity in a nation. The Civil War, according to the dominant interpretation, represented a struggle to reestablish unity, setting aside the differences found in Confederate regionalism and secession. The dominant emphasis on unity superseding diversity in these moments of national origin and testing has been indelibly written into our consciousness.

2. The Melting Pot and Robert Park

The political philosophy which shapes our view of the church was reinforced by a social model as expressed in a drama, *The Melting Pot,* penned in 1908 by Israel Zangwill. As the nation reeled under the impact of millions of immigrants from eastern and southern Europe, and conflicts emerged in neighborhoods and shops, people found their hopes for this society dramatized in vivid terms.

There she lies, the great Melting Pot—listen! Can't you hear the roaring and the bubbling? There gapes her mouth—the harbour where a thousand feeders come from the ends of the world to pour in their human freight. Ah, what a stirring and a seething! Celt and Latin, Slav and Teuton, Greek and Syrian,—black and yellow—. . . .

East and West, North and South, the palm and the pine, the pole and the equator, the crescent and the cross—how the Great

Alchemist melts and fuses them with his purging flame! Here shall
they all unite to build the Republic of Man and the Kingdom of
God. . . . Peace, peace, to all you unborn millions, fate to fill this
giant continent.[1]

The play drew great crowds from the first perfor-
mance. People longed for peace and unity which could
overcome the strains and anxieties prompted by
increasing ethnic variety. They envisioned the blending
of races in America, in which differences could be
"melted away" or "purged," and people could be "fused
together."

How does this "fusing" of races take place? In 1926
sociologist Robert E. Park formulated the story of the
"melting pot" into sociological dogma. "The race
relation cycle . . . of *contact, competition, accommodation,*
and eventually *assimilation,* is apparently progressive
and irreversible," Park stated.[2] His formulation has
become such a classic that it was detected in the
responses of United Methodists to our recent survey on
race relations.

3. E Pluribus Unum:
    An Erroneous and Undesirable Ideal

Do the negative reactions of whites to ethnically
defined structures in The United Methodist Church,
as discussed above, represent instincts shaped by e
pluribus unum, "from many one"? Does not the
majority white response to our survey mean that we
want ethnic minorities to lose their distinctiveness, and
all of us become one, if not similar or same?

Would "unity with diversity" be closer to God's
intentions? We submit that the story behind the melting
pot theory in drama or sociological dogma is an ideal

which does not explain what actually happened. In examining our situation from the perspective of our faith, we submit furthermore that *"the ideal"—the melting pot—is not even desirable for The United Methodist Church.*

In the remainder of this chapter we will present a critical review of the classical American expectation of a melting pot, and Park's theory of the progressive and irreversible process whereby ethnic minorities are purportedly assimilated into white society.

C. THE MELTING POT AND PARK: ANALYSIS

The melting pot has not become a reality in the United States, with race relations moving progressively and irreversibly from contact through competition and accommodation, to assimilation. The reality seems to have been otherwise, and the process not as continuous and inevitable as Park claims.

1. Accommodation → Assimilation: Fallacy

a. *Two-Category System: Distinct Communities.* Because of the limited extent and cost of accommodation, as well as the fallacy and cost of assimilation, transition from accommodation to assimilation purported by Park is at best a story with very little value. "Assimilation" is defined by Park and others as the process by which *people from diverse cultural and biological background join the same social groups at work, in leisure, in religious efforts, and in marriage and family.* Although some assimilation has occurred, it has not occurred as extensively as anticipated.

The extremes of reality can be seen, on the one hand,

in the unity established among the Protestants from the British Isles and Northern Europe, and, on the other hand, in the exclusion and near genocide of the American Indians. Between the two extremes is the most pervasive pattern, in which white persons remain in an upper category of advantages while the colorful people remain in the lower category of disadvantages. In housing, education, employment, income, physical and mental health, and opportunities for cultural pursuits, the majority of ethnic minorities consistently fall below the bulk of whites in resources, opportunities, and privileges.

The Kerner Commission noted in 1969 after the urban riots of the late 1960s that "Our nation is moving toward two societies, one black, one white—separate and unequal."[3] The same pattern has been uncovered with other ethnic groups. Some would call it an instance of internal colonialism, with dependency, control, and exploitation operable at many crucial points.[4] Given this recognition of distinct communities and a hierarchy between them it has become untenable to speak of assimilation without some qualifications. Thus, it is not too much to speak of a "two-category system" as the most pervasive outcome of racial interactions in this society.[5]

The same disparity is found in religious institutions. While significant ministries have occurred, the great majority of ethnic minorities often have created makeshift parallel religious institutions (black colleges, ethnic minority local churches, or subgroups within existing structures, such as ethnic minority caucus movements) which are generally relegated to a lower status, if indeed they are even observed by the dominant religious establishment.

It is important for us to realize that the development of such separate structures can represent a way of bridging the boundaries between the two sectors of our society. Without them, the predominantly white United Methodist Church would not have a mechanism to work with the distinct and expanding segment of society which racial and ethnic minorities represent.

b. *Accommodation: Not a One-Way Street.* The *accommodation* which Park predicted, also called acculturation, *is a process whereby a people with one cultural background adopts the values and behaviors of another people.* This can include language, diet, vocation, appreciation of music, and much more. Considerable acculturation has indeed occurred in the United States. Different processes, too, have been detected.

Many ethnic minorities are developing a bicultural or multicultural aspect of their identities by retaining their cultural traditions while appropriating new and different ones, or by promoting a retrieval of their cultural heritage.

Many whites, too, are developing bicultural and multicultural qualities in their religious, political, or family lives. The resurgence of Third World cultures at home and abroad, instantaneous global communications, increased travel, and mounting immigration will probably cause increased interactions between whites and colorful peoples. Thus, the one-way process of acculturation suggested by Park accounts for only a very small portion of the extensive interchanges now taking place between ethnic minorities and the white majority.

c. *Assimilation: Fallacy.* Even in critical instances where some accommodation has taken place, assimilation has not followed as suggested by Park. For example, Protestants, Roman Catholics, and Jews may share many common values and practices, but they remain in distinct and separate institutions for much of their activity. Ecumenism within the household of faith and interreligious dialogues among world religions may heighten common ventures and even lead to sharing facilities, but the religious bodies remain distinguishable.[6]

Analogously, while there is a sharing of basic commitments and collaboration in many joint efforts within The United Methodist Church, ethnic minorities have retained or are creating ethnically distinguishable structures. While all of these structures may not be acceptable to every United Methodist, it will be suggested that elements of our faith make it impossible to reject them outright.

2. Competition → Accommodation

a. *Conflicts Persist.* Park's scenario suggests that competition, tension, and strife are left behind. More recent interpretation of the "roaring," "bubbling," "stirring," and "seething" of Zangwill's play, however, recognizes the depth of the discord, the persistence of the animosities, and the painful consequences not readily buried.[7] Repressed frustrations and periodic outbursts of violence are more pervasive than accord in interracial associations, which are likely to occur in an environment of hopes deferred. Although people can still live with Zangwill's or Park's scenario and make themselves oblivious to these strains, or privileged social arrangements can shield them from experiencing the conflict, nevertheless what is recognized today is a far greater persistence of strains and violence in the interactions between groups who have been living with whites. This has been the case from the beginning of our history as a nation, such as in the cases of Native Americans and blacks. Variations on the same theme appear in the experiences of Hispanics, Asian Americans, and Pacific Islanders who entered the U.S. later.

Thus, we are led to recognize not only the persisting two-category system noted earlier, but also the added element of conflict accompanying this stratified society.

b. *The Cost of Accommodation.* There is considerable cost involved for those who subject themselves to accommodation or assimilation. They must live with an internal dialogue and occasional conflicts as they struggle for ways to live with a combination of values or to adopt new ones. Those who have experienced some amount of assimilation are often expected to be socially "ambidextrous" or socially "amphibious." That is, they are asked to work in different ways, like ambidextrous persons, using their left and right hands, or they are called upon to live simultaneously in differing social climates, like amphibious animals living on land and under water.

That is the demand placed on ethnic minority persons working in a predominantly white denomination while trying to maintain ties with their ethnic minority community. Sometimes the demanding expectation results in broken ties with their own people, or a serious deafening of their ears to a rich cultural heritage. Only with exceptional stamina and ingenuity have some of these persons retained health and sanity in their individual lives, while building stable marriages and nurturing wholesome family life. While the strains are not always recognizable, or generally acknowledged, ethnic minorities in The United Methodist Church experience varying amounts and kinds of costs required by accommodation and assimilation. Perhaps this is why ethnic persons who are willing to be subjected to such strains and tolls remain exceptions in their communities. The majority of their people who join churches are not found in mainline denominations that are predominantly white.

To illustrate the selection process which occurs before some white persons meet an ethnic minority, it is interesting to follow the selection process which enabled a Formosan to pursue graduate theological studies in the United States. Of his class of one hundred graduating from elementary school in Formosa, he was one of five allowed to go to high school. Of the two hundred in his graduating class from high school, he was one of five who could go to college. Of the five hundred in his graduating class from college he was one of two who went to theological seminary. Of his graduation class of twenty-five in seminary, he was the only one who came to the United States to continue his studies.

His example illustrates how limited is the interracial mixing that occurs in churches. The Formosan student urged the theology class to be modest about their achievements of meeting together in an even more selective educational setting. His counsel is worth remembering in almost any church circle. Vast numbers of ethnic minorities are not allowing themselves to undergo the changes required for interactions within the mainline denominations. They detect the one-way exchanges which are required: they are asked to change before they are accepted into the inner circle of predominantly white denominations, while the denomination gives little evidence that it is willing to undergo changes to receive them. It is a clear case of "you become like us, and we will like you." More and more ethnic and racial minorities are unwilling to subject themselves to this subtle but significant indignity. The costs of accommodation are too high for the dubious promise of assimilation.

3. First Stage of Contact: Prime Importance

Whether or not eventual assimilation follows contact, as Park claims, depends to a large extent on the origin of the ethnic minority involved, and at what point in our national history contact with the white majority takes place. Contacts vary, and people on both sides of the boundary between the two categories are pushed in different directions, depending on the parties involved and the time the contact occurs.

For example, if one's ancestors came from northern Europe during the colonial days, the probability of one's assimilation may differ greatly from that of a person whose ancestors came from southern or eastern Europe after the development of urban and industrial centers in the nineteenth century. It would make an even greater difference if one's ancestors came from Africa, Latin America, Asia, or the islands of the sea in the seventeenth, eighteenth, nineteenth, or twentieth centuries. The experience of people who came when slaves were needed or cheap laborers were imported would be different from that of people who came voluntarily from the middle or upper strata of a foreign society. People who came as refugees fleeing communist take-overs would be treated differently from those who became a part of this country by virtue of U.S. military action in foreign lands. American Indians discovered that it made a difference whether they came from a nation or a tribe: the obligation of whites to observe agreements with tribes was more relaxed than the obligation to observe treaties with nations!

Thus, the melting pot was true for only a very small slice of our society.

D. CONCLUSION: PERSISTENCE OF TWO-CATEGORY SYSTEM

The melting pot is not a real account of the experiences of racial minorities in the United States. Although there are some racial minorities who operate ambidextrously as they move in institutions which belong to two different categories, the promoters of the melting pot have not erased racial distinctions in the United States. This has been the grave suspicion of many ethnic minorities and is reflected in the responses of ethnic minorities to our survey. These long-standing hunches, born of prolonged struggles with their peoples, are slowly being discovered and articulated by social analysts. Stratification and conflict are pervasive and persistent. A two-category system is operating at many crucial points in our lives, with the vast majority of colorful peoples assigned to a separate lower category.

If there are distinctive communities which are defined by race, we can expect parallel institutions in churches. While activities and organizations may overlap, there are differences and distinct spheres of operation.

These are some of the major social realities which affect the structures and functions of The United Methodist Church as we try to work with ethnic minorities. Our lingering aspiration to change that pattern must take into account the dynamics at work that perpetuate various forms of the two-category system. We turn to that presently.

CHAPTER 4

Persons, Principalities, and Powers

A. INTRODUCTION: PSYCHOLOGICAL AND SOCIOLOGICAL FACTORS PERPETUATE VARIOUS FORMS OF THE TWO-CATEGORY SYSTEM

The previous chapter described cultural forces which influence race relations in The United Methodist Church. In this chapter we will consider psychological and sociological factors that ethnic minorities in our survey were eager to mention in any examination of the prospects of a racially inclusive church. We will look at the dynamics which perpetuate various forms of the two-category system. We will consider the role of individuals in multiracial exchanges; the relationship between individual attitudes and actions on the one hand, and institutions which exercise such extensive influences on our lives, on the other. While the role of individuals in race relations will be affirmed, we will also demonstrate how a broader perspective is necessary—a perspective which will lead us to engage our faith more deeply and comprehensively, and which will broaden

our understanding of multiracial experiences in The
United Methodist Church.

B. THE INDIVIDUAL IN INTERACTIONS

1. Introduction: Attitudes → Action → Consequences

Attitudes, actions, and consequences are like links of
a chain; one leads to another. It is important to
recognize the values of this perception even if we will be
led eventually to say it must be recognized as a story or
sequence of events that has limited applicability.

An illustration of how positive attitudes produce
constructive outcomes will suffice to make the general
outline more concrete. During World War II one
hundred ten thousand Japanese Americans, most of
whom were United States citizens, were removed from
the West Coast because it was feared they might
cooperate with the enemy. Eventually they were
allowed to return to their homes, but many people who
had bitter memories of the war tried to frighten them
away.

In one community, where several homes of Japanese
Americans were burned and "No Jap Trade" signs
posted, one individual played a critical role. He walked
into the shops of his hometown where "No Jap Trade"
signs were posted and simply announced that he was
removing them. One can imagine the courage involved
when such an act was unpopular. Eventually, other
efforts followed. An imaginative banker arranged with
nearby bankers to hire Japanese Americans as tellers.
As local residents did their banking, they were
confronted with a conspicuous statement. A leading
institution in the town welcomed former inmates of the

detention camps as employees. Three decades later, hundreds still celebrate an annual Goodwill Dinner which recalls the reversal of hate in their midst.

Individuals can thus play critical roles in racial tensions. In scores of neighborhoods throughout this vast land, stories of triumphs over racial tensions are told, many by the readers themselves. The solutions may not have been publicized or permanent, but for the participants in some fearsome strife, the reversal of hate was a momentous event in their shared histories. How did it come about? An individual with conviction and courage decided to act out what was astir within her or him. A course of events headed for deeper conflict and more violence was checked; neighbors again greet one another; children played safely; communities found occasions for celebration. Indeed, attitudes can prompt actions, and in turn, actions can produce consequences of considerable proportions.

While the basic outline of this story explains many interactions among races in both our society and The United Methodist Church, we are aware that other consequences take place. Let us explore alternative sequences of events by observing divergent connections occurring between attitudes and actions, between actions and outcomes.

2. Attitudes and Actions

While we assume that evil intentions produce evil acts and good attitudes result in good deeds, there are exceptions to both assumptions.[1] Sometimes persons with strong racial prejudices extend decent and good gestures despite themselves. Improvements in their attitudes could make their good deeds into better ones, but the fact remains that the gestures are good and decent. Conversely, pure motivations and goodwill are not always accompanied by informed actions. Thus, a generous, dedicated, and well-educated Christian can commit a racist act.

3. Actions and Consequences

Just as goodwill does not always produce good deeds, neither do good deeds always produce positive results. The reverse expectations are so pervasive, we must review it. Corita Kent, in *Footnotes and Headlines,* offers a memorable statement of our hope for positive results of good deeds.

> and we must be more careful
> about stamping out evil or hating anything
> because we know that in the past
> and in the present
> many people and things
> have been tragically destroyed in the name of good
> we are reminded of rilke's words
> to the young poet
> and if only we arrange our life according to that principle which
> counsels us that we must always hold to the difficult   then that
> which now seems to us the most alien will become what we most trust
> and find most faithful   how should we be able to forget those
> ancient myths about dragons that at the last moment turn into
> princesses   perhaps all the dragons of our lives are princesses who
> are only waiting to see us once beautiful and brave   perhaps
> everything terrible is in its deepest being something that wants help
> from me

The charm and legitimate hopes in such stories should not blind us to the instances when this sequence of events does not take place. Not all courageous acts turn dragons into princesses. Nor do all tender kisses of a princess turn a frog into prince charming, to recall another version of this basic story. Because we live with an overextended hope in this story of good acts rewarded with positive results, when some decent, generous, and righteous deed does not produce positive results, we are crushed.

The United Methodist Church should capitalize on the racial minorities who know profoundly that decades and centuries of patience, generosity, and faithfulness have not terminated the unloading of garbage upon their people. Their goodness did not prompt kindness, dragons were not turned into princesses. They have, however, remained loyal. As people who were injured but not destroyed, these persons represent an example of faith for the white majority as they face the mounting outbursts of human creativity in the Third World. Whites may recall numerous generous gestures through missions and foreign aid, but they may overlook the manipulations involved and the determination for independence which have been prompted.

In summary, individuals play different roles in race relations. In the first instance individuals, with right motivations, produce good actions and create positive consequences. The reverse instance is also acknowledged; evil intentions produce bad deeds and negative results. However, if we are for the moment measuring the importance of consequences, individual contributions or actions may be minimal, if not reversed. People with goodwill can perform racist acts unknowingly; people with evil intentions can act decently. Further, good acts can go unrewarded and some evil efforts can be frustrated.

Why do individuals' good motivations sometimes

result in misguided deeds? And why do individuals' good deeds sometimes not produce positive results? Some factors can be explained; others are inexplicable. Racism is a mystery at many points, touched with evasive qualities.

The considerations of this chapter concerning the role of individuals, the strange quirks of history, and the broader and enigmatic quality of racism will lead us to reflect in the next chapter on the issues of race from the perspective of faith. Unless these dimensions are dealt with in our situations, ethnic and racial minorities may well feel that the push for an ethnic presence will be an empty gesture.

C. INSTITUTIONAL RACISM

1. Plea for a Broader Perspective

When we consider acts of individuals or small groups which do not produce the results intended, we conclude that other factors must be at work. When we look for expanded causes, we find that one of the most important considerations is the role of institutions and organizations in our society, including the church.

2. Concrete Facts

A range of evidence will be reviewed. A cycle which operates in our society will determine the facts about race relations we consider. Residential patterns in large measure determine the quality of education since neighborhood schools are still the dominant pattern. In turn, these factors shape the employment obtained, income earned, and cultural patterns adopted. The resulting identities of racial minorities are used to perpetuate various discriminatory residential patterns, thus bringing the chain of cause and effect full circle. Given this cycle which plays a major role in the vast majority of racial minorities, we will review the situation in housing, education, employment, income, and cultural outlets of blacks, Hispanics, Native Americans, and Asian and Pacific peoples.

Data indicate that the impact of the most recent surge of positive and generous efforts for racial justice has been minimized or contradicted by broader social forces. The behavior of institutions has overridden the kind gestures of thousands of individuals. These wider trends play key roles in determining the ethnic composition of our local churches. Examples follow.

a. *Housing*

(1) Availability. In 1968 the national housing production goal was six million units of federally assisted housing in 1978. In each year from 1969 through 1979 the nation fell far short of construction goals; furthermore, available housing became increasingly out of reach for many citizens because of inflation and rising interest rates. According to the U.S. Commission on Civil Rights:

> As the cost of housing has escalated, more and more households headed by minorities and women are being priced out of the market. . . . Many minority and female-headed households continue to have incomes that are only about one-half the income of households headed by White males. The U.S. General Accounting Office noted that such lower income households are finding it "increasingly difficult to locate affordable rental units."[2]

Thus, not only did the country fall far short of reaching the federally funded goals, but the prices for housing rose beyond the reach of many people we tried to help. Finally, what little was available was made even less accessible by discriminatory practices.

(2) Segregation Patterns. The Civil Rights Act of 1968 contained a Fair Housing Act; the Department of Housing and Urban Development was authorized in 1969 to police housing practices. The latter produced no action; the former has been ineffective. By 1979, the U.S. Commission on Civil Rights determined that discriminatory practices continued and thus perpetuated segregated housing.

(3) Institutions Override Individuals' Positive Efforts. How do institutions override positive efforts made by thousands of individuals? Boards of realtors and member agencies assume they are protectors of neighborhood interests, and generally try to preserve residential patterns. Minorities are kept out of predominantly white neighborhoods as long as possible. When those patterns change, the institutions try to insure stopgap arrangements or make available outlets for white flight. Financial institutions are also implicated. They specify certain areas and designate certain "kinds of people" who are particularly good investments in the name of protecting those who have entrusted them with their money. Thus, very little profit is shared with ethnic minority investors; return on investment flows more to whites than to ethnic minorities. This description of the role of real estate and financial institutions illustrates the function of other institutions also involved in the housing issue, such as housing authorities, city planning agencies,

chambers of commerce, service clubs, the media, and educational institutions.

b. *Education, Employment, and Income* (Heavily dependent on housing are educational attainment, employment opportunities, and income levels.)

(1) Blacks. In 1979, a quarter of a century after the Brown vs. Board of Education decision by the United States Supreme Court, nearly half of the nation's minority children remained in isolated schools.

Correspondingly, the rate of black unemployment was on the rise when compared to that of whites. Today, the difference between the jobless rate of blacks and whites is the greatest since the federal government began keeping records of it. At the peak of the recession in 1975, the unemployment rate for blacks was a record 2.3 times that for whites, according to governmental statistics generally considered to be conservative.[3] The unemployment rate for black youth was even worse, even though their level of education was growing relative to white teen-agers. Nationally, between 1975 and 1977 the black teen-age unemployment stayed at 40 percent while the rate for white youth fluctuated from 15 to 18 percent.[4]

These unemployment statistics are related to the income of blacks. A ratio of incomes from the early years of the racial struggles to the end of the 1970s is noteworthy. In 1969, the median income of all black families was 61 percent of white families, by 1977, it was 57 percent! Contrary to much-publicized changes, the ratio of income distribution among black families in the upper, middle, and lower levels has virtually remained constant in recent years.[5]

(2) Hispanics. A survey of Hispanic employment and income profiles reveals trends similar to those of blacks. A particular fact was very crucial. Hispanics were moving into metropolitan areas where the availability of jobs was declining. While jobs were moving away from the neighborhoods being populated by Hispanics, transportation was not upgraded to make employment accessible, particularly during the late hours when services were reduced. These broad trends contributed to income patterns. In 1978, 21 percent of Spanish origin families in the U.S. lived in poverty.[6]

(3) Native Americans. The same connection between employment patterns and income distribution can be found among Native Americans. In 1976, 12.2 percent of the American Indians and Alaskan Native males were unemployed. This was twice the unemployment of white males. The percentage of unemployment among Native American women was 2.6 times that of white women. Teen-age unemployment among Native peoples went as high as 6 times that among whites. Income figures reflect this unemployment. In 1975, Native American households headed by males had a per capita median income of $2,453, or 57 percent of the income of white households. Households headed by Native American women had a per capita income of $1,310, or 35 percent of white counterparts! It is not surprising then, that 40 percent of Native American households lived at or below the poverty level, compared to 8 percent of white households.[7]

(4) Asian Americans and Pacific Islanders. *The Asian American Field Survey* of 1977 reported a study of recent arrivals among Chinese in New York City, Filipinos in

San Francisco, and Japanese, Koreans, and Samoans in Los Angeles.[8] Overall, 73 percent of these persons lived in low-income residential areas. This has clear implications about the quality of schools, hospitals, parks, shopping areas, welfare services, and transportation available to them.[9] The *Survey* noted that 31 percent of the heads of households were not in the labor force, and another 10 percent of the heads of households were unemployed. Of the men employed, 46 percent of Samoans, 44 percent of the Chinese, and 36 percent of the Filipinos were doing menial jobs. Similar statistics were noted for women.[10] The criteria for skilled workers often relegates these persons to demeaning jobs despite their extensive education upon immigrating to the U.S.[11] The poverty level of immigrants in these metropolitan areas was extraordinarily high.

3. Institutional Racism in the Two-Category System

This summary has focused on a few crucial steps in the cycle which moves through residence, education, employment, income, health, and cultural outlets. It has illustrated how the two-category system dominates crucial aspects of the lives of racial and ethnic minorities. It also reveals factors in race relations which go beyond individual attitudes and actions. Just as the person caring for plants must consider more than turning a faucet handle because the utility district, the legislature, academic institutions, and research centers determine, in their own way, what the plant is being fed, so in our personal interactions there are institutions and organizations which affect what we do to one another. We may offer an extended hand, but ingredients in our environment can transform that kind gesture into a shove. Statistics show the overwhelming effect institutions can have; statistics show that despite incalculable energies expended, monies allocated, and the painful struggles for racial justice, the inequities persist. This happens through institutions, organizations, and agencies working in housing, education, employment, and so forth—"institutional racism," it has been called.[12]

In 1947 Jackie Robinson helped open up professional sports for blacks, and became an inspiring symbol for his people, other ethnic minorities, and white people as well. Robinson did not allow his success to blind him to the work remaining for his people and in the larger society. In the year he died, he published his autobiography, concluding with these words:

> I have always fought for what I believed in. I have had a great deal of support and I have tried to return that support with my best effort. However, there is an irrefutable fact of my life which has determined much of what has happened to me. I was a Black man in a White world. *I never had it made.*[13]

Two years later, Hank Aaron received a number of death threats when he approached Babe Ruth's home-run record of three decades. The threats were only exaggerated expressions of disappointment widely felt in white communities when a national symbol is passed to a black athlete.

In some religious circles, these sport symbols may be dismissed as trivial. Even the most culturally refined among us, however, are not unaffected by such powerful symbols in the public arena. They remind us that when white boundaries are challenged, whites find themselves wondering if nothing is sacred, nothing safe from the barbarian invasions of minority peoples into sacrosanct monuments of their achievements. Thus, we observe the *scramble for new boundaries to say there is a turf where whites are safe and there is an enclosure where ethnic minorities can be contained.* Such is the subtle operation of racism at work in individuals and institutions. Now we speak of racism as a noun, a distinct entity, and not simply an adjective characterizing attitudes, actions, and institutions.

D. AN INDEPENDENT FORCE: UNCOVERING THE DEPTH OF EVIL

1. New Use of Ancient Symbols

Thus far we have determined that our efforts toward a truly inclusive membership in The United Methodist Church may be overridden by the operations of other factors in our environment which transform good deeds into injurious actions. Institutional racism may be at work.

There is, further, a resiliency in the racist behavior of institutions and racist sentiments in the most enlightened and dedicated Christians. Try as we will to exorcise these evils from our psychological makeup and to alter the racist behavior of institutions, there seems to be an inexhaustible source of new racist expressions in ourselves and institutions. We seem to be confronting something quite illusive. The problem we try to tackle slips out of our hands when we think we have it under control. It has a capacity to outwit and outmaneuver us with ever new and unexpected moves. As Robert Blauner said in his *Racial Oppression in America,* it has come time to part company with the leading ideas and implicit assumptions that until recently, at least, have guided most American social scientists in their study of . . . racial order:

First, the view that racial and ethnic groups are neither central nor persistent elements in modern societies.

Second, *the idea that racism and racial oppressions are not independent dynamic forces but are ultimately reducible to other casual determinants, usually economic or psychological.*

Third, the position that the most important aspects of racism are the attitudes and prejudices of White Americans.

And, finally, the so-called immigrant analogy, the assumption, critical in contemporary thought, that there are no essential long-term differences—in relation to the larger society—between the third world racial minorities and European ethnic groups.[14]

Blauner is suggesting, in his second assertion, that racism and racial oppression are due to an "independent dynamic force" which is not reducible to economic considerations such as greed, or psychological analyses of prejudice. As a social scientist he is voicing a belief which would not be expected from many of his colleagues. Even theologically trained sociologists would be reluctant to join him. But the results of a decade of struggling against racial injustices would indicate that he should be taken seriously.

Nor is it adequate to stop in our analysis of the issues with an abstract and impersonal appeal to "institutional racism." Blauner's suggestions move in the direction of the ancients and their mythological symbols. The ancients gave evil an independent status and thus depicted it with a body. Because of the way evil could outwit the best laid plans people could devise to trap it, and because its operations seemed too illusive, they said evil was shrewd. If evil had a body and behaved shrewdly, it was natural to depict it in a fashion reminiscent of a person, thus, the human qualities ascribed to evil in pictures and narratives. Further, because it could produce awesome and ugly consequences, evil was depicted with frightful features associated with overpowering creatures. For example, some such creatures were depicted as having human bodies and animal heads. Satan, the Devil, and their legions were never tools which could be handled, machines which could be managed. They were certainly not cute babies for cuddling or pet animals guided with a leash. They were portrayed as "independent dynamic forces," to use Blauner's suggestive phrase.

2. Demoniac Operations of the Two-Category System

Perhaps an imaginative and realistic use of ancient wisdom may lay the groundwork for uncovering the power of the gospel. Falling prey to a dull-witted scientism has incapacitated us from appropriating the wisdom of the ancients and releasing the power of the gospel.

How might ancient symbols articulate the religious dimensions of the issues we face in racism? In the previous chapters we discussed the two-category system characterizing racial exchanges in much of this society. In this chapter we added the role of institutional racism. The reason the two-category system can maintain boundaries or redefine them is the cohesiveness with which the institutions in the upper category can work together. First, a built-in backup system of various segments in the upper category is assigned to maintain various kinds of boundaries and implement diverse policies; and second, these segments work cooperatively.

One might picture the segments as columns with various layers.

The educational system offers an illustration. Happenings at the lower levels are advanced at upper levels. For racial and ethnic minorities each level of education represents a bleaching vat. With advancement from elementary school, through high school and college, the minority person is passed through every increasingly concentrated bleaching solution. Many of those who subject themselves to graduate theological education in seminaries confront a concoction which they are told comes from God, with all the sanctions and censures it entails. (The last point is raised because an overwhelming majority of the respondents in our survey felt seminaries need more sensitivity to ethnic concerns.)

This same kind of backup system appears elsewhere with minor variations. The upper category is assigned to perform the coercive measures of society, in order "to discourage evil doers and protect the innocent." People who feel themselves under the control of the upper category have differing perceptions of how it operates. Students who participated in protests against governmental policies in Vietnam, for example, uncovered such a backup system. When campus security guards could not control the situation, city police forces were called for assistance. When they proved inadequate, the county sheriff and his deputies came into the picture. In succession, the state highway patrol or troopers, the national guards, and the equipment and material from the armed services were activated. Then bloodshed. The movement was deflated like a balloon which had burst.

What white students discovered at Kent State in 1971, Hispanics discovered in Santa Fe when Reies Tijerina led a struggle in the mid-sixties; blacks in Watts in 1965; American Indians in Pine Ridge in 1973; Asian Americans in San Francisco in 1968.

This kind of backup system appears with variations in financial institutions, judicial systems, corporate structures, and the media. It is not that they perform no humane and positive function. The problem is that at crucial points the capacity to draw boundaries, or redefine them, can be activated. Levels within given segments of society can back up the lower levels. These backup systems enhance their operations by cooperating with one another. Speaking diagrammatically, the columns coalesce. For example, when Hispanics in the farm worker struggles staged a somewhat effective boycott of grapes, agribusiness found the federal government a willing partner. The United States government purchased grapes which could not be sold in the private sector and unloaded them on the armed services overseas. Thus, the column represented by federal agencies collaborated with private industry. The farm workers' struggle for organization was thus weakened, and the farmers were kept in their place. Boundaries were maintained when the highest levels of two distinct segments of this society were brought together on one issue. Such cohesiveness within the upper category when pressure is applied demonstrates its likeness to a body. There is an organic quality which can be detected in the upper category. Disparate parts are coordinated, producing very specific consequences.

To the extent that a distinct pattern of behavior can

be detected when boundaries, which regularly delineate whites from ethnic minorities, are thus perpetuated, one begins to associate personal qualities with it.
This does not suggest that the behavior is conscious and
intentional, but the behavior is regular and effective.
Those who have struggled against this system have
detected something comparable to a wit, outmaneuvering good and just intentions. The consequences of
these activities can be devastating for individual
sanity and health, for stability of families, for self-
respect, for gainful employment, and much more.
Therefore, it is understandable why such an evil
operative in a society would be depicted in ungracious
terms to put it mildly, or in frightful and hideous terms
to describe the "message of the prophets on subway
walls."

3. Peril of This Approach

To speak of the evil of racism in these terms
admittedly has its hazards and pitfalls. We can
encourage an incapacitating paranoia on the part of
those struggling against racism, whether among the
majority or the minority. We do not say that in each and
every case of racist behavior the full force of the beast
has been activated. Not all instances of racial injustice
come with columns in the upper category acting in
concert. An individual may be behaving thoughtlessly
with no malicious intent. But this admission does not
contradict the basic claim that under duress the
self-interest of the upper category is at stake, and
backup systems can be activated. If that proves
insufficient, cooperation among the segments of society
are formed when they may be otherwise quite

competitive. To deny this would be succumbing to an ailment opposite from paranoia, namely, a pollyanna perception of the world blind to significant realities affecting most minority peoples in this society and reflected in our churches.

The other hazard entailed in this approach is the danger of engendering an irresponsible fatalism among those responsible for perpetuating the evils of racism. That is, to speak of the role of an "independent dynamic force" as Blauner does, or to employ the symbols of evil powers from the ancients, seems to relieve people of their contributions toward injuries for which their racist behavior is directly responsible, thus taking them "off the hook." But those responsible must be held accountable.

4. Promise of This Approach

The total picture of human behavior, however, recognized the role of larger forces at work upon us. In the case of positive behavior, who can overlook God's enabling gift of love from someone we love? In the case of an evil such as a racist act or motivation, it would be sadly narrow if we could see only what that person is generating by him or herself. However much we may be saddened or incensed by racist behavior, or a racist person, a full understanding of the dynamics of race relations will have to include a recognition of the evils which have gathered momentum of their own once the machinery of an institution has been assembled to act in a certain preferential way. Individuals may introduce changes, but a realistic estimate of the capacities of evil would suggest that it can outwit and outmaneuver the wisest and most dedicated servant of God. If racism can prove exploitative and oppressive for racial and ethnic minorities, it can manage and manipulate the white majority.

The symbolism of the ancients suggests rightly that the behaviors of racism can continue appearing in new forms without conscious decision whether at business meetings of executive officers in institutions, or in carefully selected choices by an individual who may be prominent or little known.

E. CONCLUSION

It is not an exaggeration to say that there is an epidemic concerning racial problems in the United States. It represents the overextension of simplified analyses of the problems, which have taken on something of a religious quality and therefore exercise mystic powers: the first such analysis predicts that ethnic minorities will disappear in the melting pot; the second assures us that good feelings produce right actions and thus positive consequences. Both dreams are contradicted by the solid facts of our society. These chapters have offered alternative readings. A two-category system exists; pretenders to the throne of God exercise considerable control over the lives of racial and ethnic minorities.

Those who responded to our survey constantly referred to racism, acknowledging that these broader dimensions must be taken into account if we are to talk about racial and ethnic constituencies in The United Methodist Church. Without uncovering the depth of the evil, we would settle for a watered-down gospel. No watered-down gospel can be expected to introduce the changes required to make The United Methodist Church truly inclusive. We turn to the responses of faith to our challenge.

CHAPTER 5

"And the Fulness Thereof": The Kind of Unity God Wills

A. INTRODUCTION: NEED FOR GOD'S GUIDANCE

Prospects for racial and ethnic minorities in The United Methodist Church do not depend only on our initiating effective programs. Our efforts will be empty unless we establish more clearly how our faith may address the full dimension of the issues which confront us. In the next two chapters we will consider faith experiences that help us interpret God's actions in similar situations. They serve as clues to the present work of our creating and redeeming God, and suggest a course of action which The United Methodist Church can pursue if it is to become a faithful co-worker with God.

Respondents to our survey pointed out two kinds of pertinent faith experiences. One deals with the kind of unity God wills; the other deals with redemptive actions of this God which make such a unity possible. We will consider them in that order in the next two chapters.

Whereas the vision of heaven in some religions suggests that only a few will gain entrance, the good news of Revelation is that in heaven there will be "a

great multitude which no one could number, from
every nation, from all tribes and peoples and tongues"
(Rev. 7:9). That describes the vision many United
Methodists and other Christians have of heaven, and
the foretaste of heaven on earth, namely, the church
here and now.

As in the case of other symbols of our faith, this vision
takes on substance when seen in the context of the fuller
story of God's work. Respondents to our survey offered
various illustrations of the role of diversity in the work
of God known as Creator, as Sanctifier or Holy Spirit,
and as the Christ.

B. PROVIDENTIAL VARIETY OF CREATION

1. Secular Idea of Unity

The work of God can be seen in bold relief when
compared to the secular idea of unity in the U.S. which
has acquired religious overtones and even become a
substitute for faith among many Christians. The
Federalist model of unity was summarized in the motto
of the Republic, e pluribus unum, meaning "from many
one."

Robert Frost's poem, "Mending Wall," helps us
become aware of the ingrained propensity to move *from*
the many *to* the one. Frost writes,

> Something there is that doesn't love a wall,
> That sends the frozen-ground-swell under it
> And spills the upper boulders in the sun,
> And makes gaps even two can pass abreast.

The poet remains agnostic about the force, or Force, in
the universe which tears down walls between people,

but Christians will be quick to claim it is God who is at work. We find a wall-building God antithetical to the God we know, who surges through all the barriers set up between people and tears them down so that we can all be one.

Frost makes sport of his neighbor who builds walls out of blind obedience to some threadbare line he had been taught.

> There where it is we do not heed the wall:
> He is all pine and I am apple orchard.
> My apple trees will never get across
> And eat the cones under his pines, I tell him.
> He only says, "Good fences make good neighbors."

When we see people drawing lines of distinction within the human family, they look to us as Frost saw his neighbor.

>   I see him there,
> Bringing a stone grasped firmly by the top
> In each hand, like an old-stone savage armed.
> He moves in darkness as it seems to me,
> Not of woods only and the shade of trees.
> He will not go behind his father's saying,
> And he likes having thought of it so well
> He says again, "Good fences make good neighbors."

The tenets of civil religion are astir within us. We are asked to move away from differences, minimizing walls which delineate diversities. We are asked to become color-blind. The church teaches that color blindness is a sign of health. Thus it is little wonder that Frost's poem evokes positive reactions among so many readers. Some dark spirit moves wall-builders, he suggests, a darkness "not of woods only and the shade of trees."

But does not such a view make us work for *race erasion,* not *race relations*? When we read scripture reminiscent of the God we read about in the table of nations, we are offended. Let us examine the reactions prompted by priestly literature, which depicts God creating distinctive peoples, insuring diversity in the human family.

2. Priestly Literature: God Creates Distinctive Peoples and Insures Diversity in the Human Family

The priestly literature is associated with a period (568 B.C.E. and following) when the nation of Israel had been destroyed and the Israelites had been taken to a strange land. There they were exposed to an alien culture and faced the danger of losing their distinctive identities. Eventually a ruler permitted them to return. It was as if they had been through another flood and the creation of the children of God had to begin anew. How could they do this?

Priests took the leadership and wrote histories of their people so that a rehearsal of God's mighty acts in their midst might rekindle their unique identity. The great events of that history were vividly reenacted, in rituals, as they rehearsed their past. Priests also led those who articulated laws of behavior befitting their distinctive identity as a unique people of God. Reflections of these efforts can be found in such books as I and II Chronicles and Esther, among others.

The Books of Ezra and Nehemiah tell the stories of walls being erected around the city of Jerusalem to set it apart from the neighboring countryside. Within that city, another prominent wall was erected for a temple to designate certain places holier than others.

Minorities have experienced living in a strange land as aliens and have felt the urge to rewrite biblical stories to proclaim the mighty acts of God in the holy history of their own people—a history filled with anguish, anger, and aspirations, as well as pathos, pain, and promise. Litanies are written, songs composed, and walls repainted with new faces. These are the makings of a ritual to dramatize the gracious deeds of a God of justice and mercy.

Out of such retelling and reenactment through ritual comes a distinct identity informed by faith. Such identities can be summarized by something comparable to the priestly laws, codes of behavior which are distinctive from the dominant values associated with Christianity, in which the main lines of cultural tradition comes through Athens, Rome, Geneva, Paris, Wittenberg, London, Boston . . . , but not Africa, Latin America, Asia, the Islands of the Sea, and the indigenous voices from this native land.

Ethnic minorities who have lived through the devastations of an "urban renewal" know the tugging at the heart to hold those walls which designate areas peculiarly hallowed by grand events in a community's life—a debate, a welcome home of soldiers, a funeral procession, and much more. After destruction, the task of rebuilding is nothing less than a response to a holy calling. Such is the experience of ethnics—whether in cities, or in vast open spaces, where American Indians were removed from sacred lands to create a new sanctity within a new home.

Hence we can understand the priestly writers. To affirm the fullness of God's creation means that at many points, people will write their histories and celebrate them in rituals, summarize their identity in codes, and construct walls which designate particular places as sacred. To speak of the fullness of God's creation is to acknowledge the diversity which it contains and to recognize that God's act of creation extends into the present and covers human communities as well as the natural order. To speak of diversity is to recognize a place for those who articulate their distinctiveness. We read in Genesis 10 that the growing diversity was providential, the fulfillment of divine promise and command (Gen. 10:5, 20, 31). Priestly literature expresses the same sacred acts of this Creator God. The difference is that it is expressed in a way that challenges more directly our uncritically held faith in a unity which moves *from* a many *to* a unity.

C. THE SPIRIT RELEASES NEW LIFE

1. Unity Amidst Diversity

The God known as Creator made diversity within a single family possible (Gen. 10). The God known to us as Spirit releases new life within the diversities of the human family and creates the household of faith (Acts 2). In one church, there were diverse languages of "Parthians and Medes and Elamites and residents of Mesopotamia, Judea and Cappadocia, Pontus and Asia, Phrygia and Pamphylia, Egypt and the parts of Libya belonging to Cyrene, and visitors from Rome, both Jews and proselytes, Cretans and Arabians" (Acts 2:9-11). An enormous array! If reading the variety of unfamiliar names bewilders us, imagine the amazement when Galileans were enabled to speak this rich diversity of languages (Acts 2:7).

What is dramatized for us at Pentecost (Acts 2:44-45) is that *the God known as Holy Spirit created a unity while affirming variety in its midst!* Thus, diversity is not a curse, but a blessing. Eventually, diversity created strains and confusion, but the central message focuses on the acts of God which release new and diversified expressions of life among people.

There was resistance to God's work. Those who had known the divine actions of God in one cultural mold found it difficult to accept new and divergent expressions of faith in this same God. At that early stage of the church's growth, it was the Jewish converts to Christ who resisted the unique expression that appeared among the Gentiles.

2. Events Suggest Reversal
of Our Political Model of Unity

Several events seem critical. A few suggest a reversal of our political model of unity which is a central problem of this study. In Acts 7 we read Stephen's vision of God's work in Jewish history. There is Abraham (Acts 7:1-8), Joseph (Acts 7:9-16), Moses (Acts 7:17-44), and David and Solomon (Acts 7:45-50). Each one of these *affirmed that God could appear outside places which they were accustomed to associate with divine presence and saving work.* Abraham heard the call of God outside the Holy Land. Joseph was led out of the Holy Land and set in motion a process which later saved his family. Moses released the redemptive work of God in Egypt. He eventually erected a tent of meeting in the wilderness, for he had met God's messenger in the wilderness of Sinai. David and Solomon said that God could not be contained in buildings made with hands. Stephen, who suffered martyrdom (Acts 8:1), laid the foundation for the missionary work of Paul among Gentiles.

Joseph, Moses, and Jesus, three who reminded their people of movements of God outside familiar precincts in new peoples, suffered abuse from others. Thus, what was dramatically demonstrated at Pentecost when the spirit released new life among diverse people, is reaffirmed in different ways in Acts 7 by Stephen. He cites specific predecessors to remind his people that God's work could appear in different contexts. Some who released divine action in such settings were abused, such as the man who was "full of the Spirit" (Acts 6:3, 5).

A third incident occurs in Acts 10 when Peter was urged to set aside his inclinations to make Gentile Christians into Jewish Christians. As will be recalled, he sees "a great sheet, let down by four corners upon the earth. In it were all kinds of animals and reptiles and birds of the air" (Acts 10:11-12). When he is told to kill and eat the animals, Peter refused out of his own upbringing which had divine sanction behind it. But he is told, "What God has cleansed, you must not call common" (Acts 10:15). It took three visions to finally convince him that he "should not call any person common or unclean" and that "God shows no partiality" (Acts 10:28, 34).

We are not saying that there should be nothing in common in a denomination which has a wide diversity of racial and ethnic groups. According to Luke *those who appreciated their Jewish heritage were the ones who urged that Gentiles be allowed to express their faith in their own distinctive ways rather than adopting an alien cultural and ethnic mold.* Peter is reported to have said that God "made no distinction between us and them [the Gentiles]. . . . Now therefore why do you make trial of God by putting a yoke upon the neck of the disciples which neither our fathers nor we have been able to bear? But we believe that we shall be saved through the grace of the Lord Jesus, just as they will" (Acts 15:9-11).

Another leader of the Jerusalem church, James, epitomized an appreciation of earlier Jewish expressions of divine action. He affirmed, however, that "God first visited the Gentiles. . . . Therefore my judgment is that we should not trouble those of the Gentiles who turn to God" (Acts 15:14, 19). Even though the four conditions he stipulated were Jewish purity laws from Leviticus 17 and 18, nevertheless the overriding note is that Gentiles should be allowed to be Gentile Christians.

3. Cultural and Ethnic Issues as an Integral Part of Spiritual and Religious Issues

One cannot read the Bible in strictly spiritual or religious terms, without recognizing that cultural and ethnic issues are an integral part of the spiritual and religious issues. It is quite clear that an important issue consists of ethnic and cultural expressions of the faith. Were Gentile Christians to be asked to adopt cultural expressions of the faith that were alien to them? They were to do this only on what was then considered to be a minimum condition at best. Even these conditions were culturally determined so that they did not remain permanent in all settings (Acts 15:19-20). This is what befits us as human beings. The work of the Spirit moves through changing cultural expressions and ethnic identities.

Other passages of scripture deserve examination, such as Paul's struggles with the law in his epistles which are so central to Protestant restoration of the gospel. It is easy for us to see salvation without the work of the law—a salvation which does not demand any works of righteousness. But fundamental to this issue in Paul's Letters to the Romans or the Galatians is the cultural issue and an ethnic identity. Gentiles would not find any salvation by becoming persons they were not, as summarized in Jewish laws.

Ethnic and cultural considerations were also a part of the Reformation. They were important in the larger religious struggle when the liturgical language was changed. The question was whether Christians living north of the Alps had to become Christians as defined by those living south of the Alps. At one level this was a cultural and ethnic question, but when it became a question of power to control that decision, it became a political question.

On the surface these are cultural, ethnic, and political issues but at the core they contain religious and spiritual issues. Will the God known as Spirit violate what God known as Creator has brought into being—namely, distinctive peoples, all with their own languages, families, and nations (Gen. 10:5, 20, 31)? We are not talking simply about making ethnic minority cultures into fetishes and idols, or taking a romantic view about freezing some historic expressions of our heritage into contemporary expressions. All these dangers are involved, but the fundamental issue is whether we will contradict God's creative work. Is God of a divided mind, with the God known as Spirit setting aside what God known as Creator has providentially brought into being? Such fundamental spiritual, religious, and theological issues are being debated within the various denominations in the United States. People are asking whether racial and ethnic minorities should become white before they can become full-fledged Christians. This is only an undated version of the struggle of the early church in the "Council of Jerusalem" (Acts 15). As God the Spirit was needed then, so too in this day, the Spirit, which sanctifies even "Gentile" cultures and says that nothing is to be regarded as common or profane, has come to give new life to minorities. Praises, praises be to this gracious, embracing God!

In the Acts of the apostles, or the acts of the Holy Spirit, God the Spirit releases new life, beginning in Jerusalem, and then spreading to all Judea and Samaria, and the ends of the earth (Acts 1:8). In this cursory review of selected highlights, we have focused on the ethnic identities of people to recount the gracious and mighty acts of this God known as Spirit, confirming what we had seen in the God known as Creator. But this God as Spirit is also called the Spirit of *Jesus* (Gal. 4:6; Phil. 1:19).

D. JESUS AND THE "OTHERS"

We have seen how it is possible to speak of the Sanctifier as the *Spirit of God* (Rom. 8:9; I Cor. 2:12; 6:11), if by God we have the narrower use in mind and think it refers to God as Creator. In other words, the distinctive cultures which God as Creator has enabled to emerge, are affirmed and hallowed by God as Spirit.

But the same Spirit is also called *Spirit of Jesus,* and the Spirit of God's Son (Gal. 4:6). The reasons become obvious as we recall the work of Jesus, particularly as depicted by Luke in his Gospel. In the ministry of Jesus, as in that of the Spirit, new life is released among people different from those associated with previous works of God. The early church was saying that the God at work in Jesus was continuing as Spirit. In that sense, the Sanctifier and Consummator was the Spirit of Jesus, a continuation of the man from Nazareth.

In contrast to Luke, Matthew seems eager to depict Jesus concentrating on his own people before his disciples were sent to the world (Matt. 28:18-20). Two specific comparisons are particularly interesting. In Matthew Jesus sent the twelve on a mission, saying, "Go nowhere among the Gentiles, and enter no town of the Samaritans, but go rather to the lost sheep of the house of Israel" (Matt. 10:5-6). In Luke's mission of the twelve, no such prohibition of Gentiles and Samaritans is mentioned, nor is there a restriction to the children of Israel (Luke 9:1-6). In Luke's mission of the seventy, moreover, the field is wide open. Jesus "sent them . . . into every town and place where he himself was about to come" (Luke 10:1). Immediately afterward Jesus seems to imply that his own people in Chorazin and Bethsaida were faithless, but that "outsiders" of Tyre and Sidon repented (Luke 10:13-15).

The second comparison between Matthew and Luke concerns Jesus' treatment of the woman from Sidon. In Matthew 15:21-28, a woman from the district of Tyre and Sidon appealed to Jesus for help. Jesus said to her, "I was sent only to the lost sheep of the house of Israel" (Matt. 15:24). In Luke 4:24-27 Jesus observes that salvation had come to a widow in Sidon in a special way, and a Gentile leper was healed. Jesus startled his listeners by using as an example a military leader of one of Israel's enemies. No wonder they threatened to kill him (Luke 4:29).

Thus, in both instances Luke and Matthew's accounts of Jesus differ greatly. The Jesus of Matthew's Gospel is so intent on trying to minister to his own people that he has no time for Gentiles and Samaritans; the Jesus of Luke's Gospel includes in his ministry Gentiles, Samaritans, and many "others" who are outsiders.

Jesus will be "a light for revelation to the Gentiles," Simeon prophesies (Luke 2:32). And this he became, to the Roman centurion whose faith is held up as a model. "I tell you, not even in Israel have I found such faith" (Luke 7:9). As for the Samaritans, Luke is the only one who uses the good Samaritan story (Luke 10:30-37) and the only one who reports that one of the ten lepers who were healed, a Samaritan, thanked Jesus (Luke 17:11-19).

Similarly, Luke is compassionate toward tax collectors. Only he recounts the parable favorably comparing the tax collector's humility with the Pharisee's (Luke 18:9-14). The same is true for Zacchaeus, another uniquely Lucan story about a tax collector (Luke 19:1-10). Among those "others" who are easily forgotten are the poor. Luke recalls Jesus saying they are blessed (Luke 6:20, cf. Matt. 5:3). There is the important role of women in his narrative, beginning with Anna, Elizabeth, and Mary in the infancy narratives and continuing through the passion and resurrection accounts (Luke 1–2; 23:28, 55; 24:1, 10).

In summary, with regard to racial and ethnic groups, Luke depicts a Jesus who is particularly sensitive to the "outsiders," Gentiles and Samaritans. Among Jesus' own people, it is the traitorous tax collectors, the women, and the poor who are particularly prominent in Luke's records. *Jesus is one who releases God's saving action through these "outsiders," those who might be classified by many as "others."* Thus, in Luke the divine redemption comes to us in distinctive forms not highlighted by the other Gospel writers.

Old Testament writers remind us of God's creative work in bringing into existence unique and distinct people. The Spirit was seen giving new life, and in Jesus we see outsiders introducing God's saving health into human history. What all of this says is that a central feature of the God of biblical faith is the attention given to people in their uniqueness. What this implies for us in our consideration of ethnic minority constituencies in The United Methodist Church is that its current diversities can be enhanced if it works with this God.

E. THE UNITED METHODIST TRADITION AND THE BIBLICAL WITNESS

The United Methodist tradition is peculiarly prepared to teach this aspect of the biblical witness. One of the primary interests of The United Methodist Church has been the inner witness of the Spirit that we are children of God (Rom. 8:16). Thus, John Wesley interpreted that experience in the chapel on Aldersgate Street in London, May 24, 1738, 8:45 P.M. His heart was strangely warmed as he became aware that he did indeed trust Christ and that he was truly a child of God.

The United Methodist Church grew from a small handful of people to become one of the most vital forces in the nineteenth century and the largest denomination in the United States. We who "were not a people, . . . are now the people of God" (I Pet. 2:10 KJV).

What the sampling of racial and ethnic groups—whites and minorities alike—reveals is that the *central theological foundations for an interracial church is the conviction that we are all God's children, despite our diversity.* Society has its way of telling people that they are a lower grade of humanity, beasts of burden, freak accidents of nature, and much more. By telling people that they must become culturally different before they can belong to the church is our religious way of saying people are not fully acceptable. But the good news that is finally determinative for those who have the inner witness of the Spirit is that they are children of God. They who were no people have become people in God's sight, regardless of how they appear in the eyes of the world. To trust that word from God gives them an inner strength which enables them to stand up against all the epithets the world may hurl against them.

Thus, reflections on the issue of unity and diversity have led us back to the central elements of our faith. We have found in God's work as Creator, Spirit, and Christ the foundations for that vision of heaven and the church which captivates many of us.

I looked, and behold, a great multitude which no [one] could number, from every nation, from all tribes and peoples and tongues, standing before the throne . . . and crying out with a loud voice, "Salvation belongs to our God. . . . Amen! Blessing and glory and wisdom and thanksgiving and honor and power and might be to our God for ever and ever! Amen." (Rev. 7:9-12)

CHAPTER 6

Racism, Reconciliation, and Redemption: Enabling God's Unity to Exist

A. INTRODUCTION

The biblical and theological message is clear. God created people with diversities. Respondents to our survey gave ample witness that God not only sanctions our unique identities created in history, but also sanctifies them through the work of Jesus and the Holy Spirit. But it is not enough to speak of diversities within the human family or the church as if an affirmation of unique identities and allowance for distinct communities will automatically produce mutually beneficial interchanges. As the participants in our survey also recognize, in this society drawing distinctions fosters discrimination and creating separate structures encourages segregation. The interpreters of racial interaction characterize the resulting situation as a "two-category system." While some say that the ground is level around the cross, the results of our survey cause us to recognize the racist forces at work in our society which permeate The United Methodist Church. Most white persons are pushed closer to the cross while the majority of the minority persons are found farther away and downhill.

Respondents' comments concerning racism in ethnic interactions suggest the need for a reexamination of insights of Christian tradition concerning sin and evil. Respondents' frequent references to liberation suggest that they both recognize the permeating power of sin and evil and perceive neglected aspects of salvation. We will first discuss respondents' understanding of sin and evil, before considering the fuller salvation urged by their call for liberation. Without God's saving act, respondents believe, the prospects for an inclusive church are grim and talk about strategies is superficial.

B. SINS, SINNERS, AND SIN

The church has frequently spoken of sins, sinners, and Sin. All people commit sins and harbor sinful attitudes or feelings, thus all of us are sinners. A full understanding of human behavior and evil, however, cannot be explained fully with references to sins and sinners. Despite risks of misinterpretation and abuses of the insights involved, Christians have recognized another ingredient: Sin with a capital S. Perhaps the apostle Paul espoused this view when he said, "Now if I do what I do not want, it is no longer I that do it, but sin which dwells within me. . . . When I want to do right, evil lies close at hand" (Rom. 7:20-21).

Given the distinctive status he gives sin, and given the fact that he is drawing a parallel between sin and evil, it may be well for us to capitalize both, even if the translators have not done so. Paul also spoke of a "law of sin" (Rom. 7:23), as if sin operated in him as an inclination toward a given behavior without his initiation and intention. Since Sin is given a status distinguishable from him and yet able to work in him as a "law," it appears that Paul had something more objective in mind than we do when we pray in a hymn, "take away our bent to sinning." Those words from Charles Wesley's hymn, "Love Divine, All Loves Excelling," suggest a psychological or spiritual tendency within us not related to an "independent dynamic force."

Although the verbal parallels are not precise, we can draw conceptual analogies between these practices in Christian tradition and the dynamics of racism which have been outlined. As we speak of certain acts as sins and attitudes as sinful, so we can say certain behaviors are racist. Here "racist" is used as an adjective describing feelings and actions.

As we say persons who entertain sinful attitudes or commit sins are sinners, so we can say that those who indulge in racist feelings or commit racist acts are racists. Here the word is used as a noun. As we may distinguish between various kinds and degrees of sinners, so may we distinguish between various kinds and degrees of persons we call racists. Three classifications appear.

1. Racist by Commission

The first and most obvious is the person who may know that he or she is harboring a prejudice and acts in a discriminatory way, treating certain persons preferentially and insulting others. A person who is conscious of these attitudes and commits the deeds intentionally is a racist. Such a person represents the most pervasive use of the word "racist," applied to someone other than ourselves. Unfortunately, very few of us ever acknowledge that we ourselves are racist in this sense of the word because we can rationalize the behavior someone else calls unfair. Flailing and fuming about such racists does little to change others.

2. Racist by "Omission"

The second meaning of the word "racist" is perhaps the most applicable for persons in The United Methodist Church. Many of us are unconscious of evaluating ethnic minorities with double standards and unintentionally treating them in a discriminatory way. If we do not use the resources which are readily available and adequate to sensitize ourselves sufficiently and then to correct our own behaviors, we too are racists. Given the high expectations Jesus inculcated, how many of us have done enough with the resources at our disposal? Jesus said, "When you have done all that is commanded you, say, 'We are unworthy servants'" (Luke 17:10). Even at our best moments we would not claim to have done all that is commanded. Then how much more ought we to say with the tax collector, "God, be merciful to me a sinner!" rather than "God, I thank thee that I am not like other [persons who are] . . . unjust" (Luke 18:13, 11). We are racists because of our "sin of omission"; we have failed to use adequately the readily available resources to correct our racist behavior.

3. Racist Among Ethnic Minorities

The third use of the word "racist" is sometimes applied to racial and ethnic minorities. For example, minority persons may have allowed righteous indignation over the exploitation and oppression of their people to become a hateful attitude against any and all white persons. It may result in outbursts of vindictive and injurious action. There is no debate about the sin and evil involved. However, there is a difference between the behavior of racial and ethnic minorities, who cannot generate support from the backup systems mentioned earlier, and actions by white persons which can mobilize support from the backup system in the upper category. The statistics considered in the previous chapter suggest that despite some cooperation by several segments in the upper category (such as banks and schools) to improve the conditions of minorities in the lower category, these very systems were at the same time operating in contradictory ways which maintained boundaries. Thus, because of the vast difference in clout behind the actions of whites and those of racial and ethnic minorities, it seems appropriate to reserve the word "racist" for white persons. This is not to say that minorities cannot act sinfully in race relations by their anger, bigotry, or sickness. Nevertheless, we would exaggerate their importance by calling them racists in the same sense that term is applied to persons able to activate so much more support. As in the case of sinners, the evil may be serious and the sin obvious, but fundamental differences are important to bear in mind.

A minority person can commit racist acts. They may cooperate with the racism that oppresses their people. Biblical examples are Herod, who collaborated with the leaders of the Roman occupation, and the tax collectors who participated in an exploitative system, thus arousing the hostility of other Jews. Today, racial and ethnic minority persons in the United States who gain entrance into the upper category and court its favor can turn against their own people with disdain or worse. To the extent that their behavior perpetuates racist qualities of the social stratification, the deeds of such persons can be classified as racist. But to the extent these minority individuals can be removed whenever convenient for the upper category, their precarious status does not qualify them to be called racists in the fuller sense of that word.

This exploration into the various meanings of the noun "racist" suggests that the second sense of the word is the one most appropriate for consideration in this study. For purposes of this study a racist commits "sins of omission" by failure to take advantage of adequate resources which could possibly correct unconcious or unintentional racist behavior. Not acknowledging this can put us into the first definition of "racist" by virtue of "sins of commission."

4. Reflections: A Fundamentally Religious Issue

Why can generous and well-meaning Christians commit racist deeds? It is not enough to appeal to racist attitudes and conscious choices. "Institutional racism" is at work, which can transform a gesture by white persons toward minority persons into a collision, just as an unexpected gust of wind can throw us into the path of a friend. Yet these apparent accidents have a regularity about them. They come with such momentum and persistence that an organic quality can be observed in the problems of housing, education, employment, income, and so forth. That "body" of problems functioned so illusively, "outwitting" and "outmaneuvering" us, that a personal ascription seemed appropriate for these forces at work in our environment. Hence, Robert Blauner's "independent dynamic force" sounds possible. The theological parallel is that it is no longer appropriate to focus on sins and sinners. References to Sin and Evil become necessary. Thus we refer to Racism.

If we can speak of racist acts and attitudes as sins, racist individuals as sinners, and Racism as Sin or Evil, we are dealing with a fundamentally religious issue. We cannot dismiss race relations as a secular consideration, a social problem or a political or economic issue. All of these are manifestly involved! They are, however, infused with a religious question because of the involvement of sins, sinners, Sin, and Evil. This leads us to consider the kind of salvation offered by our faith, and the Savior who is at work.

C. SALVATION STALLED BY RECONCILIATION

1. Reconciliation: Reunion with God and Harmony Among Ourselves

If religious issues are involved in race relations, salvation is involved. It is appropriate to speak of repentance and faith, forgiveness and sanctification. For example, if we assume that certain words are harmless, but discover that they open old wounds for some persons, we can stop using them. The kind of regret and change of mind associated with repentance could promote inter-ethnic trust. If we have done some wrong, even while meaning well, we can ask God's forgiveness and forgiveness from one another. Trust in that gracious favor of other people and of God makes profound contributions to racial harmony. If our motivation for working across racial and ethnic lines was generosity mixed with self-serving ambitions, we can be sanctified by the cleansing from evil and the renewal of the right spirit within us which is associated with the Holy Spirit. Hence, the need for repentance and faith, forgiveness and sanctification, leading to salvation, and then to reconciliation. Reconciliation highlights the reunion established by salvation between ourselves and God, and the harmony we establish among ourselves within the human family. We cannot deny the authentically Christian qualities of the ingredients of salvation. Participants in our survey clearly saw this.

2. Reconciliation Alone, Short of God's Promises

However, salvation understood in these terms applies to a limited part of the total dynamics of Racism which has been uncovered. The attitudes and actions of individuals may be forgiven and changed, but it has not promised any changes in the institutional racism which can override individual efforts. Nothing has been said directly about the "independent dynamic force" which also characterizes Racism. Further, we can speak of sanctification in personal terms as a renewal of the spirit within us, and in social terms as a hallowing of distinctive identities and cultures of ethnic minorities that are created in the process of history. If we stop here we have not, however, said anything about the way the factors and forces at work in this society turn those distinctions into discriminatory treatments, separate cultures into segregated enclaves. The distinctions that we may draw in our minds may be depicted on a horizontal line but the dynamics of Racism turn them into differences that are located on a vertical line, on an inferior-superior spectrum.

What our understanding of salvation as reconciliation cannot address is the independent force of Racism which can arrange our interactions into oppressive and exploitative systems. Without deliverance from these oppressive and exploitative systems, our limited focus on reconciliation may stop us short of the fuller salvation God promises. A restricted concern for reconciliation can prevent us from moving on to redemptive qualities of salvation integral to God's work. Without redemption from these structural arrangements of institutional racism and the ideologies which validate it, reconciliation can only degenerate into appeasement or a momentary, if not delusive, relief from the alienation and subjugation. By redemption is meant a deliverance, a liberation for principalities and powers which prevail over our best efforts. Reconciliation may relieve the alienation, the guilt, and the hostility, but without the deliverance of the redemption we cannot become fully a people *of God*. We will still be managed and manipulated by forces which cannot affect the justice and mercy of God. Hence, in addition to reconciliation we need the redemptive actions of God to deliver us from the reign of principalities and powers associated wih Racism.

Making references to principalities and powers, and suggesting the operations of a host of lords, evokes negative responses in many readers. For many readers talk of Racism as an independent force presents more than the hazards and perils mentioned in chapter 4. To speak of another level of entities between ourselves and God encourages outdated superstitions, irresponsible excuses, or an acquiescence of fatalism in the face of overpowering forces. We must examine these responses before the biblical and theological foundations for a redemptive ministry can be offered.

D. BIBLICAL AND THEOLOGICAL SALVATION INHIBITED BY CULTURAL INFLUENCES

In earlier sections of this study the cultural forces that distorted our faith have been examined. In this section, we consider two cultural influences inhibiting an appreciation of the salvation recalled by our biblical and theological heritage: first, an overextended application of scientific insights and technological achievements; and second, several sociological reflections.

1. Scientific Insights Overextended

When we find dinosaur bones in a mound, we do not say God's hand placed them there. Scientific developments have taught us that such animals roamed our land. One may have fallen into a river and died, since these remains are found in sandstone which was once silt in the riverbed. The upward fold of the ground swell in that region lifted the remains into a mound. Now they can be dug up and studied. Thus, no direct appeal to supernatural forces is necessary.

Nor do we see ourselves today living under the

capricious invasion of evil spirits when we suffer a physical ailment. We do not offer sacrifices to appease the gods when we suffer a drought or have a power failure. Science and technological advancements have depopulated the heavens above. We do not look for independent forces to explain or solve these problems.

As wise as these changes in behavior and perceptions may be within their limits, it does not automatically follow that we should dismiss fully the biblical drama of salvation. Under the impact of science and technology we have become a bit dull-witted. Our ability to read with imagination ancient literature, such as the Bible, has been curtailed. We are accustomed to being literalists who look for strict correlations between the biblical text and our situation. If we find none, we dismiss the salvation stories with cosmic dimensions and participants that we do not recognize literally. Let us reappropriate these stories, taking them seriously rather than literally.

In our reflections on the dynamics of racism we seem to be up against a cohesive and persistent body of issues and problems similar to the biblical references to "principalities and powers" and "hosts of lords." Though some theologians have urged that we demythologize the Bible and remove all references to such entities and their miraculous deeds, let us explore a possible remythologizing of those accounts in order to recover the wisdom of the ancients in their analysis of evil and to reappropriate the dynamics of their witness to God's great drama of salvation. While our reference to an "independent dynamic force" may sound superstitious to some, it seems to us that without such an

acknowledgment of the working of evil we are naive
and may therefore forestall a fuller work of God.

2. Sociological Reflections: Redemption Pushed
    to the Background

There are several sociological developments which
color our perceptions of the world and history:

  a. Nationally, "we are on top of the world." We live under
the influence of a civil religion claiming that at one holy
moment in history we overturned those who reigned
over us. We declared our independence from them and
defeated the powerful agents of the king and parlia-
ment. For the better part of our history in the
nineteenth century, we lived under the shadows of
foreign powers in the Old World. We recognized that
they were powerful enough to threaten our security
and autonomy. By the time we had successfully waged
two World Wars in the twentieth century, the shapers of
our consciousness said that we were now on top.

  b. Personally, "we are on top of the poverty line." What was
true for us nationally has been true for many of us
personally. Many of us have come in one generation
from the lower strata of our social and economic ladder
and risen far higher than people once envied. In our
society, we have a poverty line defining those who are in
and those who are outside the central pool of resources,
privileges, and comfort. Other persons may be better
off than we are, but we are at least above the poverty
line. The most significant line drawn in society is below
us. Such considerations make us more conscious of
what is below us than what is above us. In a society that
lives by the myth that people move "from rags to
riches," "from the log cabin to the White House," the

sky is the limit; no barriers exist once we have broken through the poverty line.

c. Religiously, "we are no longer underground." Besides the national and personal considerations, the religious factor is at work, making it difficult for us to see anything over us. Christianity was changed from an underground movement into a recognized religion in the Roman Empire. The power of Rome was no longer an alien power working against the church but a friend and ally which protected the church and fostered its advancement. A power which had lorded it over the church from above was now a power that worked alongside, if not in many ways under, the church. This meant the alien power which had reigned above was no longer an "independent dynamic power," but was dependent on the church for its own survival. At that point in history the issue was no longer deliverance or redemption from the hostile power, but a matter of keeping peace, or achieving reconciliation with the Caesars. That alteration in the social situation shifted our understanding of salvation to reconciliation and pushed redemption into the background.[1]

Our "social status" has been shaped by stories from civil religion, our autobiographies, and the church's history. We thought we were on top and in control. We were reaching down and pulling other people up. The data, however, led us to question that high estimate of ourselves. To think there is nothing over us is a false consciousness.

Thus, if it is true that scientific and technological achievements have made us dull-witted by over-extending their valid insights, and our social status blinded us to the independent forces beyond our power of control, it may also be true that we have laid the grounds to reduce the distorting influences. Perhaps this brief discussion will enable us to acknowledge forces at work that overpower and outmaneuver us. The discussion that follows will draw special attention to the writings associated with the apostle Paul. The preacher generally depicted as summarizing salvation as reconciliation will be used to depict the redemptive ingredients of salvation as well.[2]

E. FULLER SALVATION BY REDEMPTION

This summary of the redemptive work of God will cover two topics. One will rehearse an understanding of the principalities and powers, and the second will recall what God in Christ has done about them. Once we have seen what has happened, we will turn in the next section to the calling of the church in the face of principalities and powers.

1. Principalities and Powers

There are a number of views about the world in the Bible. One that is particularly appropriate for our study is the three-storied universe with God in the heavens, humankind on earth, and the principalities and powers in between. Though the Bible teaches the recognition of only one God, other creatures between God and humankind are acknowledged—sometimes unqualifiedly, other times with hesitation. The reason is that a believer in God is so conscious of the role that God plays that all else diminishes in significance. An example of an unqualified acknowledgment of an order of beings besides God and humans is found in Ephesians 1:21, where Christ is raised "far above all rule and authority and power and dominion." An example of some hesitation in acknowledging anything other than God and people is found in I Corinthians 8:5-6. "For although there may be so-called gods in heaven or on earth—as indeed there are many 'gods' and many 'lords'—yet for us there is one God . . . and one Lord, Jesus Christ, through whom are all things and through whom we exist."

Ephesians 6:12 offers a moral evaluation: "For we are not contending against flesh and blood, but against the principalities, against the powers, against the world rulers of this present darkness, against the spiritual hosts of wickedness in the heavenly places." The passage is particularly pertinent for race relations. There can be no doubt about the role of people in perpetuating Racism. Blacks clearly acknowledge "the Man" as the critical problem in the oppression of their people. In the late sixties, after the outbursts of urban protests, the Kerner Commission concluded in words which became something of a litany of confession concerning human culpability.

> What white Americans have never fully understood—but what the Negro can never forget—is that white society is deeply implicated in the ghetto. White institutions created it, white institutions maintain it, and white society condones it.
>
> White racism is essentially responsible for the explosive mixture which has been accumulating in our cities since the end of World War II.[5]

Although the phrases "white society,". . ."institutions,". . . and "racism" may have an impersonal, abstract quality, it is clear they refer to people. This study does not wish to overlook human responsibility, but it also argues that for a full understanding the mystery of evil cannot be overlooked. One way to articulate that illusive, resilient quality is to invoke the symbol system which was suggested by Blauner's phrase, "independent dynamic force." The biblical symbol system uses such words as "principalities," "powers," "dominions," "gods," and "lords" when referring to specific and concrete entities. The illusive qualities are captured in such words as "spiritual hosts" in Ephesians 6:12.

In some passages that independent dynamic force is expressed as an ideal that is destructive to people. The apostle Paul, for example, spoke of the law as the "elemental spirit of the universe" making people into slaves (Gal. 4:3). By "law" he meant that summary of the moral life articulated by his Jewish heritage. Although he was profoundly appreciative of this law, he was also appreciative of cultural differences in the wider Hellenistic world, and recognized that these moral norms could become cruel standards for others. He wrote in Romans 7:12, "The law is holy, and . . . just and good." The law, however, could also become a curse to Gentiles, or an instrument of death. Paul recognized that Gentile Christians would not find salvation by living up to ethical norms that Jewish people developed in their interactions with God. Hence, salvation "from the law" or salvation "without the works of the law" should not be generalized into an attack on any moral codes. The context for such phrases in the writings of the early church reminds us to keep the ethnic issue in focus. Racial and ethnic minorities must not be asked to become other than what the providence of God created for them.

In light of Luther's total work, we observe that a fundamental issue at stake in the Reformation was the ethnic identities of Christians in Germany. Would Luther and his people become Latins before they became fully Christians in the presence of God, or would they become fully Christians with only their German cultures that God gave them? The Reformation supported the latter alternative, which was supported by the New Testament. Later, when a conflict between Christians in the British Isles and Rome came to a head, the same issue was involved, along with the political, economic, and social issues. The new branch of Christendom called the Anglican Church made explicit the ethnic considerations involved. They were Anglicans, not Roman Christians.

A sad and sobering observation can be drawn. In the early church the Hellenistic Christians were not accepted by Jewish Christians, so separate structures had to be created. In the same way the Germans were not accepted by Latins, nor Anglicans by Romans. Divisions emerged because of the failure to create adjustments which would incorporate diversity within a single church. Likewise, when people, made marginal by industrialization and colonialism, could not fit into the Anglican Church, a Methodist denomination came into existence. Will ethnic minorities be forced to create their own church if they are to give unique witness to the divine presence in their distinct identities and cultures? The point is that a split was caused when the

law, which summarized the particular genius of people
and the specific gifts God gave them, became a norm for
others. The "elemental spirits of the universe" (Gal. 4:3)
enslaved the Gentiles. Salvation thus included deliverance from these alien spirits or laws (Rom. 10:4).

In these various ways, the Pauline witness is clear.
Principalities and powers can emerge between humankind and their God. Individuals, institutions, and
ideologies move into position and usurp the role of the
Almighty as guide and guardian. People are no longer
God's people; they belong to something less than God.
These hosts of lords, being less than God, cannot
deliver the truth, the strength, the love, and the life
associated with God. Falsehood, animosity, and death
become the prevailing and pervasive qualities of human
interaction. Such is the biblical picture of the problem
we face. Salvation means not only that animosities will
be reduced through reconciliation, but also that people
will be delivered from the conditions which create
animosities and the forces which perpetuate these
conditions. Only when Jesus prevails over principalities
and powers can we expect to become God's own people.

2. God Liberates Through Christ:
   "Already," "Not Yet," "Then"

It is the work of Christ which makes this happen.
Jesus was accused of working with the Evil One because
he violated so many of the norms which had been
hallowed by tradition. He met with women of ill-repute,
ate with traitors who collaborated with Roman imperial-
ism, worked on days when even God rested, and
predicted the destruction of the sacred precincts. When
his enemies accused him of being an agent of the Evil

One, he reminded them, "A house divided against itself
. . . will not be able to stand" (Mark 3:25). He claimed
his work amounted to taking over the reign of the Evil
One who held the territory securely before his work
began. "When a strong man, fully armed, guards his
own palace, his goods are in peace; but when one
stronger than he assails him and overcomes him, he
takes away his armor in which he trusted, and divides
his spoil" (Luke 11:21-22; Mark 3:27; Matt. 12:29).

Christ is depicted as one on the offensive. He suggests
that those who follow him would storm the stronghold
of evil. The very "gates of hell shall not prevail" against
the onslaught of those who proclaim Jesus as the
Promised One, the Christ. His teaching drove out
darkness, and his healing and exorcism drove out the
Evil One which had occupied people's spirits, souls, and
bodies. The drama one gathers from the records is that
on the cross, the Evil One pitched a last ditch stand and
hurled the full armament upon Jesus. In death Jesus
entered the citadel of the Evil One. But through death,
new life was released; death could not contain him.
Thus, one who lives in trusting and vulnerable service
to God becomes an avenue of new life. In the death
upon the cross, Jesus "disarmed the principalities and
powers and made a public example of them, tri-
umphing over them in him" (Col. 2:15). In the
resurrection, God "raised him [Jesus] from the dead
and made him sit at the right hand in the heavenly
places, far above all rule and authority and power and
dominion, and above every name that is named. . . . He
has put all things under his feet" (Eph. 1:20-22).

Jesus is *already* Lord, so that "at the name of Jesus every knee should bow, in heaven and on earth and under the earth, and every tongue confess that Jesus Christ is Lord, to the glory of God" (Phil. 2:10-11).

While the New Testament speaks of Jesus already being Lord, can we not also acknowledge that he is *not yet* Lord because he has yet to bring all things under his reign? That tension was acknowledged in Hebrews 2:8. "'Thou [the Creator] hast crowned him [Jesus] with glory and honor, putting everything in subjection under his feet.'" Now in putting everything in subjection to him, he left nothing outside his control. As it is, we do *not yet* see everything in subjection to him" (Heb. 2:7*b*-8, italics added).

In the interim, the one who epitomizes love, faithfulness, life, and truth should work to make such qualities the prevailing and pervasive qualities.

> "Sit at my right hand,
> till I make thy enemies
> a stool for thy feet." (Heb. 1:13, from Ps. 110:1)

Beyond the *already* and *not yet* there is *then*. The early church witnessed to a time when the reign of God would be fulfilled. The reign of usurpers who could not deliver the truth, justice, mercy, and love of God would be replaced by the God who is all these qualities. "*Then* comes the end, when he [Jesus] delivers the kingdom to God . . . after destroying every rule and every authority and power. For he must reign until he has put all his enemies under his feet" (I Cor. 15:24-25, italics added). That is when "the kingdom of the world has become the kingdom of our Lord and of his Christ, and he shall reign for ever and ever" (Rev. 11:15).

The story of salvation which God has accomplished in Jesus calls for both imagination and faith. Imagination does not mean flights of fantasy. We are called to see a work accomplished in the "already," a work underway in the "not yet," and a work which will be completed "then." We are called to find our place within that story in our own lives.

Christians have by tradition located themselves in the "not yet," between the "already" and the "then." We boldly proclaim that Jesus is *already* Lord of hosts over the hosts of lords. Because parts of creation which have gone awry are not wholly under control of his goodness, Jesus is *not yet* fully Lord. When the goodness of Jesus pervades all, *then* he will have delivered the reign to God and destroyed the evil rules, the illicit authorities, and the destructive powers. Meanwhile the reign of principalities and powers must be overturned and brought under the reign of God. The pretenders to the throne of God must be dethroned and subjected to the pervasive presence of God's truth, justice, love, and life. Until God is the penetrating and pervasive quality in all of us we will not be God's people.

If we see the work of God in Jesus in these terms, we acknowledge that God is not simply our reconciler, but our redeemer as well. Our deliverance from the reign of principalities and powers will bring about a mutual reconciliation between minority and majority peoples. Harmony will not require us to blind ourselves to the stratifications of the two-category system. When we live under the reign of God we will not be managed, manipulated, outwitted, or outmaneuvered by the "independent dynamic power" of Racism.

But we must remember what remains unfinished. Jesus, by trusting and vulnerable service, moved offensively into the stronghold of the Evil One, and disarmed the principalities and powers. Such service prompted a backlash which eventually meant an abusive life and an ignominious death. Through it, however, God unleashed an unending life which brought health and salvation to all. We, like Jesus, are called to promote the reign of God over the usurpers, to facilitate the reign of the Lord of hosts over the hosts of lords, including those we find in Racism.

The fullness of God's work cannot be released in our world today unless these redemptive dimensions of salvation are included with reconciliation. If Jesus does not save us from such principalities and powers, we have reduced him to a trivial savior. If Jesus is not the Lord of hosts over the hosts of lords, we have reduced him to a puny lord of some small manor. Let not the people called United Methodists truncate the great promise of God. Let not the people called United Methodists profane the mighty name of Jesus, which means Savior, our respondents urged.

These rehearsals of the mighty acts of God in Jesus have already given some clues to the mission of the church. Let us make the implications explicit.

F. THE CHURCH IN MISSION: OVERTURNING THE "HOSTS OF LORDS"

A segment of nineteenth-century Protestantism in the United States that related social reform to

revivalism illustrates the way the church can faithfully
continue the biblical stories of salvation associated with
the work of Jesus. The movements, of which the United
Methodist heritage was a part, contributed to the
combination of personal regeneration and social
salvation among revivalistic reformers.[4] Their battles
against slavery of blacks provide graphic historic
examples of combining personal conversion with social
activism. This was reflected in the questionnaires of this
study and implied in the fuller picture of salvation
outlined above.

A supporter of Charles G. Finney (1792-1875), the
Oberlin revivalist and opponent of slavery, wrote him a
letter saying, "We live, brother Finney, in a wonderful
age. What mighty *overturnings* both in the moral and
political world! I am expecting some astonishing
overturnings of God, both in the church and state, the
world over."[5]

An urgency drove the combatants against racial
injustice. The turmoils in their society were the tremors
of divine indignation moving toward the overturn of
exploitation of blacks in their society. The author of
Uncle Tom's Cabin (1852), Harriet Beecher Stowe,
warned "This is an age of the world when nations are
trembling and convulsed. A mighty influence is abroad,
surging and heaving the world, as with an earthquake.
And is America safe? Every nation that carries in its
bosom great and unredressed injustice has in it the
elements of this last convulsion."[6]

These socially sensitive evangelicals were realistic
about the resistance which vested interests would

unleash upon promoters of fundamental social changes. Samuel Harris, a college president turned theological professor, foretold ingredients of the conflict.

> Christ's kingdom is not responsible for the violence and revolution which are incidental to the epoch of its progress are occasioned by the opposition of the kingdom of darkness. . . . Any epoch in the progress of Christ's kingdom is liable to encounter violence and bloody opposition, and the advancement of Christ's kingdom may be in the midst of revolution and confusion.[7]

Because these nineteenth-century revivalistic reformers saw themselves working under the reign of principalities and powers, they worked for the "overturning" of evils so that the Lord of hosts might prevail over the hosts of lords. They realized that the hosts of lords would not surrender graciously but would eventually wage a violent resistance. The reformers anticipated the suffering that would result in working for outward changes in society. We are not surprised at the inward changes that would be required within individual Christians to be faithful to this larger picture of God's salvation.

The point of beginning for the church's struggle for liberation and the meanings of the end in "overturnings" need further explorations. Because these nineteenth-century reformers of the church's mission saw themselves beginning *from below,* that is, *under,* the reign of principalities and powers, they were not suffering the cultural blinders that made them think they were "on top of the situation." That perception of their beginnings made possible a fuller picture of their task.

An interpretation of the work of Jesus describes the two possible meanings of overturning as the church's mission. When the apostle Paul speaks of Jesus putting "all his enemies under his feet" (I Cor. 15:25), we picture him rising over principalities and powers, *subjugating* them to the reign of love, justice, mercy, and truth of God. According to this interpretation, the intermediaries have not been destroyed, but evils have been exorcised from them. In the same passage, however, we read of Jesus *destroying* principalities and power (I Cor. 15:24).

Both interpretations can be applied to human experiences. Evils are exorcised from individuals when new insights and sensitivities humanize their interactions with others. Institutions with improved policies and new personnel can mean positive changes. Alterations can be introduced into an ideology or ethos of a culture and thus improve social climate for women, persons with handicapping conditions, and racial and ethnic minorities. All these examples can be seen as exorcising evils from individuals, institutions, and ideologies which have played an oppressive and exploitative role. In this way, they are brought under the reign of the will of God.

Some principalities and powers, however, have not simply been subjected to God's will; they have been destroyed. Royalty as a way of governing nations no longer exists except in a symbolic form in Europe. Nor does the "divine right of kings" hold any sway among

the ideologies for ruling societies. Slavery no longer
exists as it did in the seventeenth and eighteenth
centuries. Thus, overturning hosts of lords can be seen
as either exorcising evil from individuals, institutions,
and ideologies, or as destroying them. Both are
consistent with the Bible and history. Both depict the
church's calling.

Though one system of slavery may be destroyed,
other forms of enslavement can emerge. Thus, we live
in the *not yet,* while longing for the *then.* Albert Camus
depicted this challenge in a story about a city
struggling against the plague. When the plague had
finally run its course, the people celebrated jubilantly.
Dr. Rieux, who battled the siege, found it difficult to
join them.

> As he listened to the cries of joy rising from the town, Rieux
> remembered that such joy is always imperiled. . . . The plague
> bacillus never dies or disappears for good. . . . It lies dormant for
> years and years in furniture and linen-chests. . . . It bides its time
> in bedrooms, cellars, trunks and bookshelves. . . . The day would
> come when, for the bane and the enlightening of men, it would
> rouse up its rats again and send them forth to die in a happy city.[8]

Respondents to our survey acknowledged that to be
Christian is to recognize that the pestilence of racism
"can rouse up its rats" even in the church, the "happy
city" of God on earth. At the same time, these same
Christians affirm the depth of God's work. All
bedrooms, cellars, trunks, and bookshelves will be
eradicated of the pestilence that sets neighbor against
neighbor. God will make it possible for the whole
human family to gather. "A great multitude which no

one could number, from every nation, from all tribes and peoples and tongues" will be there.

In the interim, God will grant some foretaste of that grand moment. We now explore the steps which might make the glimmerings of that inclusive company possible in our midst.

CHAPTER 7

Means to the Ends

A. INTRODUCTION:
FOCUS ON THE LOCAL CHURCH

We have surveyed the historic visions and early moves toward an inclusive body of believers in The United Methodist Church. We have examined the mounting impediments Racism puts in the way of those hopes and recalled the mighty acts of a creating and redeeming God which compel us to explore avenues to the realization of that historic vision.

We limit ourselves to the local church as the arena for action. As Bishop A. Raymond Grant observed, "The problem of racial segregation infects [United] Methodism at every level of its institutional life. . . . Nowhere is the problem more agonizingly stubborn, however, than at the local church level." If the barriers to the wholesome Body of Christ are peculiarly intensified in the local church, so is the possibility for change. At least that is what we read in the 1980 *Book of Discipline*.

It is primarily at the level of the local church that the Church encounters the world. The local church is a strategic base from which Christians move out to the structures of society. It is the function of the local church to minister to the needs of persons in the communities, where the church is located, to provide appropriate training and nurture to all age groups, cultural groups, racial groups, ethnic groups, and groups with handicapping conditions as minimal expectations of an authentic church. (Par. 202)

Directing attention to the local church does not suggest that God's work and our calling do not include other avenues. Problems of racism and possibilities for change exist at other levels of The United Methodist Church including Annual Conferences, general boards and agencies, colleges and universities, hospitals, facilities for the aging, service centers for children and youth, and scores of community centers and organizations. Yet the peculiar role of the local church recognized in the 1980 *Book of Discipline* justifies our focus on it without suggesting that other arenas of the church's mission are not involved.[1] We will examine three basic patterns of local churches: (1) the ethnic minority local church, (2) white local churches, and (3) racially mixed congregations.

B. THE ETHNIC MINORITY LOCAL CHURCH

1. Role

The ethnic minority local church is the Missional Priority of the 1977-80 and 1981-84 quadrennia. Responses to our survey indicate a high appreciation for the unique role of the ethnic minority local church in this society. Numerous roles played and being played by these churches are deeply meaningful to our respondents.

a. Support During Crises of Life. Who was present at our births and gave us enabling names in baptism that would withstand all the degrading names we would hear later in life? Who confirmed that we had come of age when society treated us like children needing guidance? Who sanctified our unions in marriage and visited us when we were sick, in prison, or destitute? Who hallowed the painful departures when death darkened our homes? The local church is the only institution that has been with us during those times of life when the ground seemed to shift under us.

b. Community Services. Between the moments of crisis, the ethnic minority local church has provided a range of community services unmatched by any other institution. The local church has been a quasi-housing authority, a makeshift employment agency, an *ad hoc* immigration office, and a legal aid society. It has offered supplementary education when public schools fell short of their promise and private schools were out of reach or closed to racial and ethnic minorities. It created social and recreational outlets when other programs had no room for us.

c. Sustaining Force of Life. The local church nurtured and sanctified the music we composed, the poetry we wrote, and the images we painted when concert halls, literary societies, and museums snubbed our creative work. It trained the leaders who stand tall before the people. These churches were mutual aid societies when the bank failed in that role. When morticians would not handle our dead, we organized our own funeral societies around the church. When darkness fell upon our people, the church lit a candle so we could find our way. When light broke on the horizon, the church consecrated that moment with a celebration and a deepened call for the long haul ahead. The ethnic minority local church may have been slow, and often weak when it finally took up a cause, but in its totality, it has been the most consistently sustaining institution in our communities.

d. Potential. Other than their local church, there are few institutions in this society which racial and ethnic minorities can truly call their own. Sociological facts concerning their indigenous leadership and support suggest that they are likely to continue mobilizing their communities. Who can say what the Spirit will use in the future? With the momentum of its tradition and its community organizations, the ethnic minority local church is likely to play a critical role in the mission of God in the days ahead.

2. Contributions to The United Methodist Denomination

The importance of the ethnic minority local church for its people is considerable. What of its contributions to The United Methodist Church?

a. Infusion of Life and Dedication. First, it offers the denomination an infusion of life difficult to find elsewhere. The leadership of these churches knows the profound hurts that racism can inflict. Even after those who bear the name of Christ injure them, they remain faithful, while many whites run away from minorities when their interactions become painful.

An Hispanic clergywoman's struggles and determination to work in the church were shaped by a

memorable story which she reported in the question-
naire for this study. "Cecil Williams said a few years ago
. . . that he was so hurt by segregation in the church that
he has always wanted to strive for a church whose doors
would be opened to all persons, no matter who they are
or what they do . . . my fantasy would be a church of this
kind." The Reverend Cecil Williams, a black United
Methodist, has indeed helped create such an inclusive
church at the Glide Memorial United Methodist
Church in San Francisco, California. He, with additional leaders at the church, has extended the outreach
ministries of Lizzie Glide, whose bequest helped launch
the church. When the Reverend Mr. Williams was hurt
by segregation, did he leave the church? No. Why have
thousands of other minority persons not left the
predominantly white denomination? Because they
believe that the church is of God, and not owned by a
particular people. Is this not a love, a loyalty, a
dedication, and a hope against hope, needed by The
United Methodist Church at this point in its history?

   *b. Help in Bridging Gap Between The United Methodist
Church and the Third World.* There is a second
contribution which the ethnic minority local church has
to offer. It can help the overwhelmingly white
membership of The United Methodist Church develop
ties with a growing racial and ethnic minority population which is increasingly becoming "off limits" to most
whites. Through such ties, The United Methodist
Church could interact with the resurgent Third World,
which is now the vast majority of the human family. The
Third World is increasingly taking the initiative in
world development and by the year 2000 will represent

the majority of the household of faith as well. While ethnic minority Christians are not the exclusive means of interacting with the Third World, their potential is generally overlooked by the church. In their efforts abroad, white church leaders play "leapfrog" over United States racial and ethnic minorities who are directly affected by such developments abroad and those at home. It is at considerable loss of potential contribution that we United Methodists overlook such persons at a time when mission interaction has become a central ingredient in global outreach.

3. Variety of Racial and Ethnic Minorities

The United Methodist ethnic minority local church includes an enormous variety of persons—blacks, Hispanic Americans, Native Americans, and Pacific and Asian Americans. Even within each of the groups, there is immense diversity. Variety among blacks is created by geographic differences, their place in societal and economic levels, length of residence in one location, and much more. Over three hundred nations, or "tribes," exist among Native Americans! There is a difference in ministry to those in rural settings and to those in cities. There are differences in missionary work among the three Hispanic groups—those with Mexican, Cuban, and Puerto Rican ancestry. In addition, there are other Central and South American ancestry groups in this country.

A vivid illustration is seen with Pacific and Asian Americans. The four traditional national ancestry groups among Asian Americans—Chinese, Japanese, Koreans, and Filipinos—are now diversified with additional groups, including Southeast Asians, Vietnamese, Laotians, Thais, Malaysians, Indonesians, and Cambodians, who are often Kampucheans. There is a growing number of Southern Asians from India, Sri Lanka. At the same time, people from Hong Kong distinguish themselves from Singapore Chinese, as do the Taiwanese (Formosans) from those in mainland China. Although we speak of Asian Americans, Pacific Islanders are reminding us of their distinct identities despite cooperative efforts in housing, education, employment, and United Methodist caucuses. Thus, the long phrase, "Asian Americans and Pacific Islanders," or "Pacific and Asian Americans," conceals a bewildering diversity of cultural identities within one ethnic group. Any sensitive and imaginative work with these people, who may someday be called Pacasians, must take into account social differences, the importance of generations, religious affiliation, and much more.

4. A Few Guidelines

a. Sensitivity to Cultural Heritage. The great diversity of racial and ethnic minorities in the United States alerts us as United Methodists to a wide range of possible types of ministry. Our survey elicited responses that may give some guiding principles. How can we develop and strengthen the ethnic minority local church which appears to be so crucial? Respondents consider it very important that ethnic minority local churches be sensitive to the cultural heritage and ethnic identities of their communities.

b. Worship and Clergy: Crucial Importance. For drawing

in and nurturing adults in understanding and commitment for service and stewardship, the moment of celebration and proclamation in various groups and in diverse settings appears to be the most effective means. No function of the church ranks so high with such consistency as does the life of worship. Respondents suggested these reasons: the distinctive music through which the Spirit takes hold of lives; the direct and compassionate word proclaimed in the language of the people; prayers of praise amidst the darkness and anxieties of life; some confession which cleansed and renewed; a thanksgiving which brought new life; a desperate cry of intercession or supplication; a reading of the Word which gave direction and opened a new dimension of life; the reenactment of the sustaining story which answers the human question: Will God indeed make a dwelling with us on earth? Yes, we are told, and more. God descended into the depth of hell and neutralized the forces of evil on us and the cosmos!

Respondents reflected an acknowledgment of the crucial difference clergy can make in worship, notwithstanding the critical role played by the laity, the district superintendents, bishops, and general boards and agencies in sustaining these local efforts. Appreciation for the role of the minister is accompanied by serious questions in all ethnic groups (whites included) concerning the adequacy of the training which seminaries and schools provide local pastors. Respondents expressed the belief that many persons are effective *despite* their training! They carry with them cultural qualities that training may not enhance, and more likely than not, it attempts to repress or erase them.

With our history, this focus on celebration should not surprise us. The United Methodist heritage's spread of the gospel depended very heavily on worship in its ever-changing forms. Camp meetings and revivals, with their creative departures and continuing embodiment of Christian practice, are cases in point. Thus, in developing and strengthening ethnic minority local churches or insuring the continuation of communities which undergird and serve others, the act of worship plays a peculiarly crucial role. When through a given leader, either lay or clergy, the redeeming and empowering work of the Spirit is released, a community of hope and action, of love and service, comes into being.

   c. Human Services. Let us not overlook other avenues for developing and strengthening the ethnic minority local church within the predominantly white United Methodist Church. Service in the full range of human needs was highly appreciated by respondents, and was named as one reason for the strength of the ethnic minority local church, in addition to its solid religious foundation. The ethnic minority local church fulfills the need for friends of like age or gender, for the language of love from someone during a trip through the valley of the shadow of death or the peaks of human experience, or simply for food, shelter, and clothing. The message of respondents in our study is clear: churches which do not address these basic issues have no integrity.

   d. For Children and Youth: Educational, Social, and Recreational Programs. For children and youth the educational, social, and recreational programs are particularly important.

This summary of observations and experiences of respondents in the sampling may provide white members a framework within which they can channel their participation and support.

C. ETHNIC MINISTRIES
IN WHITE CHURCHES

We turn from a consideration of ethnic minority local churches to ethnic minority ministries which local churches with a predominantly white membership can conduct. Possible efforts include workshops on white racism, incorporation of the contributions of ethnic minorities into various programs of the white local churches, and cooperation with ethnic minority congregations in the mission of the church. Each avenue will be explored.

1. Racism Workshops

Since racism operates with particular effectiveness through white institutions, workshops on racism are particularly helpful to white congregations. Racial minority participation and leadership would be appropriate, as well as leadership from the growing number of whites whose understanding of racism may prove illuminating. A workshop with a particular focus can be very effective. The Indian Heights United Methodist Church in Overland Park, Kansas, for example, examined how racism can work through the educational programs of the church. Church school teachers and officers had sessions on the literature and audiovisuals used in the program, the language they spoke, the images which guided their behavior, and the "body language" which speaks louder than words. The same type of workshop could be conducted for ushers, or for lay members and clergy who work with ethnic minority persons at Annual Conference committee sessions.

The guiding principle is to deal with racism in concrete situations of our ministry, to avoid the proverbial "paralysis of analysis" of racism in the abstract. Racism workshops can be conducted before, during, and following interactions with ethnic minorities. The important point is *that some concrete action be related to the workshop,* such as welcoming ethnic minorities to a worship service, studying about them in a women's circle or class, going to a joint camping program, or visiting an ethnic minority local church and neighborhood.

2. Incorporating Ethnic Minorities and
   Their Contributions Into the Work
   of a White Congregation

A second form of ministry helpful to our efforts to overcome Racism deals with the incorporation of the contributions of ethnic minorities into the work of a white congregation.

The United Methodist Missional Priority recognizes that racial and ethnic minorities are

> persons with a history of being exploited, oppressed, and neglected, but who have a rich heritage of culture, life-style, and theological insight. [Their] churches historically have not been accepted as a full part of The United Methodist Church, and therefore the denomination has not benefited from the rich heritages represented in these churches.[2]

With racial and ethnic minority leadership a white congregation could explore ways to incorporate these rich minority heritages into evangelism, worship, education, outreach ministries, group work, and stewardship.

For example, the worship of local white congregations might highlight the contribution of racial and ethnic cultures to *The Book of Hymns* as well as to the supplements which are being offered in *Songs of Zion* from the blacks and the Asian hymnal from Pacific and Asian Americans.[3] Similar resources are being prepared for the educational ministry of the church.

Resources thoughtfully introduced into the ongoing life of the church's ministry can have an impact. The persons whom they represent should also become a part of that resource and ministry. This calls for at least periodic visits of racial and ethnic minority persons to white local churches, and ideally the incorporation of minorities into the ongoing ministry of the denomination in such roles as lay leader and diaconal or ordained clergy. The United Methodist Church has already taken a stand on the "open pulpit." Open itinerancy of ordained clergy is an established policy.[4] When racial or ethnic minority ministerial leadership is appointed to a predominantly white-membership local church, a workshop to facilitate cooperation between the local church and the ethnic minority clergy would be helpful.

Incorporating racial and ethnic minority contributions through continuing minority presence and leadership represents a very promising avenue toward an inclusive United Methodist Church. There are other important concerns. The historic conflicts concerning the language used in worship, or *The Book of Worship,* which is considered as authoritative, is one such issue. A group in the English church argued in effect that God spoke with peculiar clarity and acted with marked effectiveness through *The Book of Common Prayer.* Other sixteenth-century Christians belonging to the same church found that requirements to use a single resource could not be tolerated. They founded the "free church" tradition of which we are in part heirs. Puritans have gone to the gallows arguing for the right to use other resources than *The Book of Common Prayer.*

Thus, we should not be surprised if there is stiff resistance to God's saving action coming through other than familiar modes of worship, education, stewardship, or mission. We can prompt unnecessary conflict by proceeding in an unthinking and heartless fashion. And yet we cannot avoid all conflict when we are touching a fundamental issue about God's work. This applies even on matters as apparently innocuous as arrangement of altar flowers. Asian altar flowers are quite different from European ones. A discussion of their meanings and spirituality could raise basic questions about witnessing to the holiness and beauty of our God.

A predominantly white denomination associated with the minority of humankind simply cannot isolate itself from other modes of receiving and expressing God's presence and work. The life and work of The United Methodist Church can be enhanced by the ministries of the racial and ethnic minorities in its midst as they draw upon the distinct contributions which the

Third World offers and which the Missional Priority encourages. This emphasis can help express religiously the multiculturalism which growing numbers of white United Methodists are experiencing in work, travel, and intermarriages. For a mission which appropriates as well as shares, the requirement of bilingual skills for white ordained ministers for Annual Conference membership is not unrealistic. After all, we have expected immigrant pastors to have skills in English and their native languages.

3. Mutuality in Mission Between Two Churches

Beyond workshops on white racism and efforts to incorporate ethnic minority contributions, white local churches can engage in various forms of "mutuality in mission" with ethnic minority local churches. This may take the form of collaboration in an ethnic minority local church's special ministry, either within its own program or a venture by others in their community, such as tutorials for youth, on-the-job training in industries and professions, or day care centers for infants and children. Senior citizens may be looking for outlets through which to serve or may be seeking services for themselves and their friends. No white congregation can say it has no mission field in ethnic ministries. An inspiring model of two districts, one in Michigan and the other in New York, has been reported.[5] Clergy and lay have traveled across many states to support each other in mission.

Such ventures should not be divorced from workshops on white racism, since partnership in mission can evoke subtle but harmful forms of condescending paternalism and maternalism. Collaborative effort will require study, joint planning, continual assessment and adjustments, and a context of worship. The context of worship cannot be overlooked, for our work interacts with worship. We are not simply changing our psychological makeups, or social conditions. This is the work of God. Service refers to action and to prayer. Prayers relating to our work include adoration of God, confession of our sins, thanksgiving for God's grace, supplication and intercession, patient listening, and acts of surrender and commitment.

There are other forms of racial and ethnic minority ministries which white congregations might adopt. The three basic forms have been suggested from the sampling of the survey. These samplings are only "pump primers." A "pump primer" is a small amount of water poured into a pump to create a vacuum which will draw water from the well. It is hoped that this brief summary will bring refreshing ideas to white local churches which will water a field hungering for imaginative ethnic minority ministries.

D. RACIALLY INCLUSIVE CONGREGATIONS

1. Those in Transition

The racially mixed church appears in various forms. The first form of racial mixture is a temporary one appearing in churches undergoing transition, usually from white to black, sometimes to Hispanic or Asian American. *Racial Transition in the Church* by James H. Davis and Woodie W. White places local church work in the broader context of the community.[6] It offers illuminating scenarios to help local leaders understand their situations and guidance for their efforts.

2. Those Permanently Inclusive

In the second form of inclusive church, the racial mixture may be more permanent. While changes in racial composition are realistic expectations historically, there are other possible outcomes.

a. Overlapping Communities. There are some overlapping communities, despite the overriding two-category system, and some local congregations reflect this mixture. For example, in San Francisco every predominantly white church has a dozen to fifteen ethnic minority members. Considering the many small congregations in the city, such numbers can be significant. The same pattern is likely to appear in other metropolitan areas.

b. Intermarriage. Another reason for relatively permanent racially mixed congregations appears in the patterns of intermarriage. Currently from 70 to 75 percent of the Japanese and Chinese Americans are marrying outside their national ancestry groups. The pattern is growing in other ethnic groups. If local churches are to reflect the social realities of their communities, we can expect these interracial families to become a part of racially mixed churches.

c. Sharing Facilities with Another Congregation. The practice of sharing the facilities of a single church building by several racial and language groups is becoming widespread both in urban and rural settings. Much experimentation is underway at the point of organization, scheduling, lay and ministerial leadership, and funding.

All three forms of racially mixed local churches bear watching and deserve encouragement and support.

E. CONCLUSIONS

We have explored various ways of increasing the racial inclusiveness of The United Methodist Church through the local church. Our heritage characterizes us with this practice and hope at several historic points of departure. The challenges were considerable in the beginning. They are mounting. They could prove to be insurmountable for the denomination.

In our earliest moments, a ready openness and a modest start toward inclusiveness could be detected, but social currents and historical events overruled easy advances. The slave economy, the Indian Wars, and invasion of the Southwest and the islands in the Caribbean and the Pacific, and the importation of Asian laborers—to name the more conspicuous symbols—eventually produced separate categories for racial and ethnic minorities in this society—categories which have been reflected in the church. Very few of those associated with the lower category could be found in mainline white denominations associated with the upper category. The very traits which qualified racial and ethnic minorities for membership and leadership in the major denominations, jeopardized their ability to relate to the majority of their own people who were found in the lower category.

But God had done what is necessary to redeem those whose dreams for an inclusive human family have been overridden. In Christ, these evil powers are disarmed and overturned. We see the Spirit releasing the "first fruits" of those possibilities which Christ has made vivid to us.

The United Methodist Church can be one such first installment, which the Bible calls the "earnest of the Spirit." The fuller realization is depicted in that grand vision, where we can look and behold "a great multitude which no [one] could number, from every nation, from all tribes and peoples and tongues, standing before the throne and before the Lamb, . . . crying out with a loud voice, 'Salvation belongs to our God'" (Rev. 7:9-10).

As the "first fruits" and the "earnest of the Spirit," The United Methodist Church can at least bear witness to that fuller outcome, even if it cannot embody it totally. Thus, both in our local churches where that inclusiveness may appear momentarily or for long periods, and in our denomination as a whole, with its variety of ethnically distinct local churches, we can give witness to that great drama. The fullness God created may have gone awry, but God is unrelenting in the redemption of that richness. A realisitic estimate of our task has uncovered immense barriers. But if the very gates of hell cannot prevail against the advances of God's redemptive work, our labor is not in vain. Thanks be to God. Amen.

Notes

Chapter 1
1. *The Book of Discipline of The United Methodist Church* (Nashville: The United Methodist Publishing House, 1980), p. 20.
2. Alan K. Waltz, "The Number of Lay Members of United Methodist Churches in Racial and Ethnic Groups," 1973: as cited in Sarla Lall, *Background Data for Regional Strategy Development* (New York: National Division of the Board of Global Ministries, The United Methodist Church, October, 1980), p. 23.
3. A. Raymond Grant, quoted in Peggy Billings, *Segregation in The Methodist Church* (Cincinnati: Board of Missions, The Methodist Church, 1967), p. 16.

Chapter 2
1. Wade Crawford Barclay, *History of Methodist Missions.* Part One, *Early American Methodism, 1769-1844.* Vol. I, *Missionary Motivation and Expansion* (New York: The Board of Missions and Church Extension of The Methodist Church, 1949), p. 15.
2. John H. Graham, *Black United Methodists: Retrospect and Prospect* (New York: Vantage Press, 1979), pp. 10-11. Dr. Graham cites two sources: W. T. Watkins, *Out of Aldersgate* (Nashville: Department of Education of the Board of Missions of The Methodist Episcopal Church, South, 1937), pp. 48-49; and Wade Crawford Barclay, *History of Methodist Missions.* Part One, *Early American Methodism, 1769-1844.* Vol. II, *To Reform the Nation* (New York: The Board of Missions and Church Extension of The Methodist Church, 1950), p. 2.

3. Carol V. R. George, *Segregated Sabbaths: Richard Allen and the Emergence of Independent Black Churches, 1760-1840* (New York: Oxford University Press, 1973).

4. Graham, pp. 3-5.

5. Graham, pp. 6-11; William R. Cannon, "Education, Publication, Benevolent Work and Missions," in *The History of American Methodism,* Vol. I (New York: Abingdon, 1964), pp. 589-90; and Barclay, *Missionary,* p. 123.

6. W. Richey Hogg, "The Missions of American Methodism," in *The History of American Methodism,* Vol. III (New York: Abingdon, 1964), pp. 60-62.

7. *The Book of Discipline of The United Methodist Church* (Nashville: The United Methodist Publishing House, 1980), p. 69.

8. Barclay, *To Reform a Nation,* p. 71.

9. Frederick A. Norwood, *The Story of American Methodism: A History of the United Methodists and Their Relations* (Nashville: Abingdon, 1974), p. 115.

10. D. K. Flickinger, *Our Missionary Work from 1853-1889* (Dayton: United Brethren Publishing House, 1889), p. 120. Readers should consult the section on "Rights of Racial and Ethnic Minorities," in the Social Principles, *The Book of Discipline of The United Methodist Church, 1980,* Par. 72 as well as "A Charter for Racial Justice Policies in an Interdependent Global Community," "Persons of Japanese Ancestry," and "Relationship with American Indian Movement," in *The Book of Resolutions of The United Methodist Church,* edited by United Methodist Communications (Nashville: The United Methodist Publishing House, 1980), pp. 38-42, 177-78, 185-86, and 222-23 for additional references to earlier resolutions still in effect.

11. James P. Brawley, *Two Centuries of Methodist Concern: Bondage, Freedom, and Education of Black People* (New York: Vantage Press, 1974), especially pp. 55-155.

12. Sarla Lall, *Background Data for Regional Strategy Development* (New York: National Division of the Board of Global Ministries, The United Methodist Church, October, 1980), p. 23.

Chapter 3

1. Israel Zangwill, *The Melting Pot: A Drama in Four Acts,* revised edition (New York: Macmillan, 1939). Originally published in 1909, pp. 184-85.

2. Robert E. Park, "Our Racial Frontier on the Pacific," in *Race and*

Culture (New York: The Free Press, 1950), p. 149. Originally appeared in *Survey Graphic,* LVI (May, 1926), p. 150.

3. *Report of the National Advisory Commission on Civil Disorder* (New York: Bantam Books, 1968), p. 1.

4. Colonialism as an analytical model for race relations in the U.S. is applied to our history in Graham C. Kinloch's study, *The Dynamics of Race Relations: A Sociological Analysis* (New York: McGraw-Hill Book Co., 1974), especially, pp. 6, 9, 121-25, 201-9. Robert Blauner, in *Racial Oppression in America* (New York: Harper & Row, 1972), applied the model to recent decades. His footnotes provide a guide to the extensive literature, primarily related to blacks. For the use of "internal colonialism" as an analytical model for Mexican Americans, see, for example, Rudolfo Acuna, *Occupied America: The Chicano's Struggle Toward Liberation* (San Francisco: Canfield Press/Harper & Row, 1972), pp. 237-41; Richard Gardner, *Grito! Reies Tijerina and the New Mexico Land Grant War of 1967* (New York: Harper & Row, 1970), and E. Ludwig and James Santibanez, *The Chicanos: Mexican American Voices* (Baltimore: Penguin Books, 1971), pp. 16-20. The approach was adapted to Native Americans in *The Navajo Nation: An American Colony* (Washington, D.C.: U. S. Commission on Civil Rights, 1975). Samples of Asian American uses of internal colonialism appear in *Roots: An Asian American Reader* (Los Angeles: Asian American Studies Centers, 1969), edited by Amy Tachiki.

5. Roger Daniels and Harry H. L. Kitano, *American Racism: Exploration of the Nature of Prejudice* (Englewood Cliffs, N.J.: Prentice-Hall, 1970), pp. 5-28, and Harry H. L. Kitano, *Race Relations* (Englewood Clifs, N.J.: Prentice-Hall, 1974), pp. 47-48.

6. See Will Herberg's *Protestant—Catholic—Jew* (Garden City, N.Y.: Doubleday & Co., 1960. Revised Edition) for a sample of this approach.

7. See *Violence in America: Historical and Comparative Perspectives, A Report to the National Commission on the Causes and Prevention of Violence, June, 1969,* prepared under the direction and authorship of Hugh Davis Graham and Ted Robert Gurr (New York: New American Library, 1969), pp. 43-91 for an historical survey. William M. Newman, in his *American Pluralism: A Study of Minority Groups and Social Theory* (New York: Harper & Row, 1973) concludes that conflict must be a major category for analysis. He writes, "Conflict has been chosen as an organizing

concept here both because it has been one of the most overlooked aspects of majority-minority relationships in previous theories and because it appears to be a central phenomenon in this kind of society," p. 183.

Chapter 4

1. The discussion which follows will offer a limited validation of the psychological approach to race relations while enlarging it with a sociological orientation. The psychological approach is illustrated in two classical studies, one focusing on prejudice, and the other on authoritarian personality traits. For the former, see Gunnar Myrdal, *An American Dilemma* (New York: McGraw-Hill Book Co., 1974) and Gordon Allport, *The Nature of Prejudice,* abridged edition (New York: Doubleday & Co., 1958); and for the latter, see Theodore W. Adorno, et al., *The Authoritarian Personality* (New York: Harper & Brothers, 1950). Joe R. Feagin is particularly helpful in recognizing the limited value of a psychological focus for social interaction. See his *Discrimination American Style: Institutional Racism and Sexism,* jointly authored with Clairece Booher Feagin (Englewood Cliffs, N.J.: Prentice-Hall, 1978), pp. 2-15, and his *Racial and Ethnic Relations* (Englewood Cliffs, N.J.: Prentice-Hall, 1978), pp. 11-17. Also useful in placing the various approaches in their context is Graham C. Kinloch, *The Dynamics of Race Relations: A Sociological Analysis* (New York: McGraw-Hill Book Co., 1974), pp. 71-127; and Roger Daniels and Harry H. L. Kitano, *American Racism: Exploration of the Nature of Prejudice* (Englewood Cliffs, N.J.: Prentice-Hall, 1970), p. 12, where they distinguish between prejudice, a psychological focus, and other broader concepts, such as discrimination, segregation, confinement, expulsion, and extermination.
2. *The State of Civil Rights, 1979: A Report of the United States Commission on Civil Rights* (Washington, D.C.: U. S. Government Printing Office, January, 1980), p. 9.
3. Bureau of Census, U. S. Department of Commerce, *Social and Economic Status of Black Population in the U.S.: An Historial View, 1780-1978* (Washington, D.C.: U. S. Government Printing Office, June, 1979), Special Studies Series, p. 23; No. 80, Current Studies Reports, p. 175, 201. Robert Hill, *Black Families in the 1974-75 Depression* (New York: National Urban League, 1975), p. 77.
4. *Black Population,* p. 188.

5. *Black Population*, pp. 31, 184; Hill, p. 14.

6. *Current Population Reports (CPR), Populations Characteristics, Persons of Spanish Origin in the United States: March 1978* (Washington, D.C.: U. S. Government Printing Office, June, 1979. Series P-22, No. 339), p. 12; and U. S. Commission on Civil Rights, *Improving Hispanic Unemployment Data: The Department of Labor's Continuing Obligations* (Washington, D.C.: U. S. Government Printing Office, May, 1978), pp. 4, 8; and U. S. Commission on Civil Rights, *Puerto Ricans in the Continental United States: An Uncertain Future* (Washington, D. C.: U. S. Government Printing Office, October, 1976), pp. 57, 61.

7. Urban Associates, Inc., *A Study of Selected Socio-Economic Characteristics of Ethnic Minorities Based on the 1970 Census, Volume II: American Indians* (Washington, D.C.: Department of Health, Education, and Welfare, July 1974), "We, the First Americans," (Washington, D.C.: U. S. Government Printing Office, June, 1973), p. 10; U. S. Commission on Civil Rights, *The Navajo Nation: An American Colony* (Washington, D.C.: U. S. Commission on Civil Rights, September, 1975), especially pp. 21-56.

8. Canta Pian and Keewhan Choi, *Asian American Field Survey* (Washington, D.C.: U. S. Government Printing Office, 1977).

9. *Ibid.*, p. 8.

10. *Ibid.*

11. Tom Owan, *Asian Americans: A Case of Benighted Neglect and the Urgent Need for Affirmative Action* (Washington, D.C.: HEW Publications, NO. (OS) 75-121, 1974), pp. 40-41.

12. Louis L. Knowles and Kenneth Prewitt, eds., *Institutional Racism in America* (Englewood Cliffs, N.J.: Prentice-Hall, 1969).

13. Jackie Robinson, *I Never Had It Made* (New York: G. P. Putnam's Sons, 1972), italics his.

14. Robert Blauner, *Racial Oppression in America* (New York: Harper & Row: 1972), p. 2, italics mine.

Chapter 6

1. Gustav Aulen, *Christus Victor: An Historical Study of the Three Main Types of the Idea of Atonement,* translated by A. G. Herbert, reprinted with an introduction by Jaraslov Pelikan (New York: The Macmillan Co., 1969); H. E. W. Turner, *The Patristic Doctrine of Redemption: A Study of the Development of Doctrine During the First Five Centuries* (London: A. R. Mowbray, 1952); Jaroslov Pelikan, *The Christian Tradition: A History of the Development of Doctrine,* Volume I, *The Emergence of the Catholic*

Tradition (100-600) (Chicago: University of Chicago Press, 1971), especially pp. 121-55.

2. Werner Georg Kummel, *The Theology of the New Testament: According to Its Major Witnesses, Jesus, Paul, John,* translated by John E. Steely (Nashville: Abingdon, 1973), especially pp. 185-93.

3. *Report of the National Advisory Commission on Civil Disorder* (New York: *The New York Times,* 1968), pp. 2, 11.

4. Timothy L. Smith, *Revivalism and Social Reform in the Mid-Nineteenth Century* (Nashville: Abingdon, 1957) and William G. McLoughlin, *Revivals, Awakenings, and Reform: An Essay on Religious and Social Change in America, 1607-1977* (Chicago: University of Chicago Press, 1978).

5. Quoting Dirck C. Lansing, in C. C. Cole, *The Social Ideals of Northern Evangelists* (New York: Columbia University Press, 1954), p. 3, italics added. In *The Redeemer Nation* (Chicago: University of Chicago Press, 1968), Ernest Lee Tuveson says the hope for a thousand year reign of the saints over evil forces depicted in Revelation 20:1-3, produced the "doctrine of 'overturning'" (p. 98). He quotes Enoch Pond who wrote in his *Kingdom Given to the Saints* (1843) that Christ "will overturn, and overturn, and overturn—till intemperance and war and oppression of every kind . . . all those multi-form evils which now afflict the earth and insult the heavens, shall be taken away." See Tuveson, p. 98, note 6.

6. As quoted in Ernest L. Tuveson, *The Redeemer Nation* (Chicago: University of Chicago Press, 1968), p. 190.

7. Tuveson, *op. cit.,* p. 83. Tuveson observes: "Although spiritual change is an essential element in the transformation of the world the Antichrist is so well dug in, so closely allied with great temporal rulers, that his overthrow will be 'violent.'" See Tuveson, p. 70.

8. Albert Camus, *The Plague,* translated by Stuart Gilbert (New York: Modern Library, 1948), p. 278.

Chapter 7

1. The "operational manual" for the 1981-84 Missional Priority, entitled, "Developing and Strengthening the Ethnic Minority Local Church" (Evanston, Illinois: United Methodist Communications, 1981), also focuses on the local church but includes suggestions for a number of other arenas for action. A packet, entitled "Horizons and Promise: The Ethnic Minority Local

Church," has also been produced by United Methodist Communications. Additional resources are forthcoming from boards and agencies.

2. Quoting the "Emerging Directions Document" of the General Council on Ministries, 1978, in "Developing and Strengthening the Ethnic Minority Local Church," p. 9.

3. In "EMLC: Reflection, Study, Action," prepared by Dorothy Turney-Lacy, additional resources published by the Board of Discipleship are listed for use in study and worship. In "A Service of Worship," prepared by the Reverend Readus J. Watkins, reference is also made to the *Dakota Indian Hymnal.* Both items are included in the packet mentioned in note 1, above.

4. *The Book of Discipline, 1980,* par. 527.

5. The effort is reported by Delton H. Krueger in "EMLC Missional Priority: Creates Expanded Horizons," included in the packet mentioned in note 1, above.

6. James H. Davis and Woodie W. White, *Racial Transition in the Church* (Nashville: Abingdon, 1980).